Studying
the Ancient
Israelites

Studying the Ancient Israelites

A GUIDE TO SOURCES AND METHODS

| | | | | | | | | | | |

VICTOR H. MATTHEWS

Baker Academic
Grand Rapids, Michigan

© 2007 by Victor H. Matthews

Published by Baker Academic
a division of Baker Publishing Group
P.O. Box 6287, Grand Rapids, MI 49516-6287
www.bakeracademic.com

and Apollos
(an imprint of Inter-Varsity Press)
Norton Street
Nottingham NG7 3HR, England
email: ivp@ivpbooks.com
website: www.ivpbooks.com

Printed in the United States of America

Library of Congress Cataloging-in-Publication Data

Matthews, Victor Harold.
    Studying the ancient Israelites : a guide to sources and methods / Victor
H. Matthews.
        p. cm.
    Includes bibliographical references and indexes.
    ISBN 10: 0-8010-3197-4 (pbk.)
    ISBN 978-0-8010-3197-7 (pbk.)
        1. Jews—Civilization—To 70 A.D. 2. Jews—History—To 70 A.D.
3. Palestine—Civilization, Ancient—Historiography. 4. Palestine—
Historical geography. 5. Bible. O.T.—Antiquities. I. Title.
DS112.M335 2007
933—dc22   2007020967

British Library Cataloguing in Publication Data
A catalogue record for this book is available from the British Library.
UK ISBN 978-1-84474-225-7

Contents

Introduction

There is a curious imbalance between the large number of reference and textbooks available on the Bible and the relatively small number of volumes that deal with the world of the ancient Near East. This sometimes gives the impression that the Bible was created in a social vacuum, despite the many references to other peoples and nations. Certainly, there are many reasons, both theological and historical, why it is important to know what is in the Bible. It is, however, equally important to study the world of the ancient Israelites within its literary, social, and historical context. This volume is therefore designed as a sort of hybrid focusing on the biblical and ancient Near Eastern sources and anthropological, geographic, historical, literary, and sociological methods that will make the study of the ancient Israelites more complete.

But why do we want to communicate with another culture—especially one that is separated from us by a vast gulf of time and space? In the case of ancient Israel, the answer to this question is based on a number of factors. One, of course, is the strong interest in the Bible as an essential element in so much of our society's thinking and beliefs.

Modern literature is filled with references to biblical stories or characters, and many of the values expressed in biblical law are still being debated by politicians. Furthermore, the society that is featured in and that helped to produce the Bible had an enduring influence on the development of three great religious movements—Judaism, Christianity, and Islam. Yet another reason for a close study of ancient Israel is to be found in our fascination with the ancient world in general, with archaeology and the findings of excavators throughout the world of the Bible. Unfortunately, it is no longer possible to make a live field study of the ancient Israelites, nor can we visit their villages and towns to interview them, to examine their homes and workshops, or to analyze their everyday behaviors as eyewitnesses. The ravages of time and the destructiveness of the elements and the subsequent human inhabitants of their lands have extinguished all hope of completely reconstructing their world. Therefore, in order to attempt a practical study of the ancient Israelites it is necessary to take into account these limitations and to take stock of what scholarly tools best facilitate this endeavor, for it is in the synthetic task of putting together a plausible picture of an ancient culture that we come to grips with its origins and development and thereby come to understand its particularities as exemplified in the received text or the unearthed artifact.

Thus the purpose of this volume is to provide a guide to the study of the world of the ancient Israelites that can serve as a supplement to larger textbooks or provide guidance for personal study as a companion to the Bible or to gain a better understanding of the issues that are voiced and the disputes that still drive the political situation in the Middle East. By applying scholarly tools to biblical material and artifactual evidence, we will have a better chance of creating a synthetic picture of the ancient Israelites that will help us navigate through some of the challenges encountered when looking at particular details. Since its focus will be broader, although less detailed than an atlas, a history, or an introduction to the Old Testament/Hebrew Bible, it can more efficiently introduce students to the tools and data available for studying the ancient Israelites and their social context. Some attention will also be given to why such a study can become contentious and controversial. The intent here is not to take sides, but rather to describe the tensions, being respectful of all perspectives. By providing readers with an orientation to the study of the ancient Israelites, this volume can place them on a better footing for navigating these controversies. In other words, it is intended to be a starting point and hopefully a catalyst for further study and investigation.

Navigating through the Sources

One of the most important considerations when writing a book is deciding to whom it is being addressed. If I were writing exclusively for scholars, I would make certain assumptions about their training and level of knowledge, and I would employ a much more technical style and vocabulary. In this case, however, my intended audience is students, laypeople, and their instructors. With that in mind, I do not want to bog readers down with an overly technical approach, and at the same time I do not want this to be so elementary that it fails to provide the coverage necessary for further research and study. As a result, in each chapter I carefully explain the methods used by scholars in a variety of disciplines and discuss the artifactual and textual remains that have survived from antiquity. I also try to make this more user-friendly by creating a large number of insets and sidebars that summarize or highlight information. To indicate my sources and to aid further research, I provide select bibliographies at the end of the first and last chapters, plus a comprehensive reference list at the end of the volume.

The other consideration in writing is mapping out the text. During the process of putting this book together, I rearranged the chapters several times while trying to decide exactly where my starting point should be. In the end I decided on a path that literally would take the reader from the ground up. Thus I will present the world of the ancient Israelites by first taking the readers through the basics of historical geography. We will then turn to archaeology and see how its values, limitations, and excavation techniques contribute to a reconstruction of life in the ancient Near East. A look at the various literary methods that have been developed over the last century will assist us in a more effective reading of the Bible. Moving from physical artifacts to social context, we will employ sociological and anthropological theories to suggest how customs, traditions, legal pronouncements, and the biblical narrative contribute to a better understanding of their social world. Taking us back to available sources, a brief summary of the history of the ancient Israelites also deals with the issue of historicity as it relates to the Bible and ancient Near Eastern records.

Chapter 1: Historical Geography

What do topography, ecology, and climate have to do with shaping the culture and identity of ancient Israel?

I begin with a chapter on historical geography, but this is not a dry litany of facts and strange place names. Instead I address here one of the chief deficiencies of students— not being able to visualize the physical stage upon which ancient Near Eastern history and biblical events took place. Even in the face of the tumultuous events occurring today in the Middle East and the Gulf Wars, few are really aware of how ancient cultures and their history have been shaped by the character of the terrain in their respective regions.

Although I do intend to provide a basic orientation to the physical geography of the region, my intent is primarily to make it clear how the ancients viewed their world. They created geographies, both physical and ideal, that were part of their national identity. For instance, to say that Israel's dimensions extended "from Dan to Beersheba" (1 Sam. 3:20) or "from Lebo-hamath to the Wadi of Egypt" (1 Kings 8:65) makes perfect sense to the ancient audience, but leaves us scratching our heads, not only because of the unfamiliar terms but because these boundaries do not, as we understand it, match the actual political borders of Israel. Instead, they reflect the Israelites' understanding of the Promised Land, regardless of more practical considerations. This tells us that complexities have been pushed aside in favor of a catchphrase that bolsters national pride or provides a sense of inclusiveness.

I also intend to spend some time examining biblical narratives to determine how they can help us understand life in a Mediterranean climate where the physical resources (ability to harvest two crops if rains are sufficient, ability to grow olive trees and grape vines to produce cash crops) or their deficiencies (lack of deepwater harbors on the coast of Canaan, denuded hillsides, and badly eroded slopes) govern what is possible. While it may not sound exciting to discuss the scenery of the stories, it is a truism that the set provides not only the backdrop but also the mood for the play.

Chapter 2: Archaeology

How does archaeology contribute to the study of the ancient Israelites?

Once a basic familiarity is achieved in placing the Israelites within their geographic and environmental setting, our focus will shift to the scientific tools available for studying the physical remains of the cultures of the ancient Near East.

There is a popular myth that the veracity of the biblical account can be proven by archaeological discoveries. Let me assure you that it is very unlikely that the next shovelful of dirt lifted from the ancient tells in Israel or Palestine will provide absolute proof of the events in the Bible. The reality is that archaeology has real limitations, chief of which is the destructive nature of time, the elements, and successive inhabitants of the region who systematically reused building materials and dug pits through ancient occupation layers. I myself have discovered that it is not unusual for an archaeologist to very carefully remove layers of soil within a measured square and suddenly discover a pair of broken sunglasses mixed in with Roman pottery.

In this chapter I intend to provide a basic description of modern excavation techniques and the artifactual evidence produced by modern fieldwork. Central to this discussion will be the statement that archaeology is neither intended to prove nor capable of proving the biblical narrative to be correct. It deals with the material remains of a succession of ancient cultures. While these physical objects appear to be only mute testimony to the activities of the ancients, they can be read and reflected upon, literally "listened to" in the sense that they serve, in much the same way as the biblical text, as artifacts of the culture that produced them.

After I have described the techniques employed by archaeologists, I will then concentrate on the way in which they interpret the data that is discovered in the excavation process. Attention will be given to the major artifactual remains: ceramics, architecture (domestic and public), tombs, and extrabiblical inscriptions. In each case, I will discuss not only the nature of these artifacts, but how they fit into the overall picture of interpretation. The conclusions that are drawn here indicate that even though real evidence illuminates the material culture of the peoples who once inhabited ancient Canaan, Philistia, Transjordan, Phoenicia, and Syria, a complete picture is not possible, and conjecture is often more typical of archaeologists than hard and fast conclusions.

Chapter 3: Literary Approaches

What insights into ancient Israelite culture can come from a critical study of the Bible and the literature of the ancient Near East?

It may be easiest to draw a reader into the world of the ancient Israelites by starting with what is most familiar, the biblical text itself. Of particular interest to many readers of the Bible is simply the narrative and how it functions as an indicator and shaper of both ancient and modern cultural values and development. Since the Bible is an artifact of ancient Israelite society, it can be studied as a body of ancient literature and can be divided up into various literary genres (i.e., short story, poetry, song, prayer, proverb). Using these familiar literary labels can help a modern reader to better identify with the material. It also allows the reader or scholar to work with the "received text," that is, the version of the text that we now consider reasonably authoritative based on the work of text critics and translators.

However, the Bible is not the only textual artifact available for our study of the ancient Israelites. Since the late nineteenth century, the Bible has come under greater scrutiny as other pieces of literature, law, and political pronouncements have been uncovered by archaeologists in the Middle East. This has resulted in a wide variety of analytical and comparative approaches, examining these various texts as part of the social milieu of the ancient Near Eastern world. Literary, legal, and theological parallels have been identified, but, as always, caution must be taken in making too broad generalizations. Furthermore, since the Bible survives in manuscripts that date no earlier than the second century BCE, careful attention must be given to the genres represented in the text, the forms and editing of the text, and the influence of the canonical process, as the text's relevance shifts for various audiences and faith communities. These methods, in turn, allow us to apply social categories to the events described in the narratives and, hopefully, to make those stories come alive for modern readers. In this chapter I will introduce several of these methods and provide examples from both the biblical narrative and some ancient Near Eastern texts that will demonstrate how they work. I do not intend to advocate one particular method over another. I think that they work best as a scholar's "toolbox" and can be used separately or together to draw meaning from the text and thus contribute to our study of ancient Israel.

Chapter 4: Social Sciences

How can the social sciences help us reconstruct the world of the ancient Israelites?

Given the limitations of archaeology and the growing body of social-scientific methods (ethnoarchaeology, anthropology, sociology, and psychology) that have been developed to analyze modern cultures, it is appropriate to utilize these methods in the service of our task. While it must be understood that these techniques also have their limitations and must be used carefully so that they do not predetermine the social reconstruction of elements found through excavating ancient sites and the biblical text, their usefulness has been proven over the past three decades. Of course, ancient Israelite culture no longer exists, and its members cannot be observed or interviewed to obtain firsthand information on their reaction to biblical narratives or about their everyday life. As a result, reconstruction of their emic ("insider") viewpoint becomes a matter of interpretation and is subject to the degree of objectivity that the researcher can apply to the text and to available archaeological data.

In order for the outsider to even begin to reconstruct an emic perspective based on the artifactual remains of an ancient culture, certain recognizable social terms, concepts, and values must become a part of the process. The etic ("outsider") interpreter then can make claims about cultural acts as described in the narrative or extrapolated from examination of a physical artifact. Although this is never an entirely objective process, the data can be refocused and its meaning clarified on a sort of universal cultural scale. What I hope to demonstrate is that even though we cannot fully understand the ancient Israelite emic perspective on beliefs and actions, there is still a possibility of deriving insights into what the "insiders" can tell us about their world.

Therefore, once the methods have been discussed and defined in this chapter, I will ask a series of significant questions that are designed to show how the methods can be used in conjunction with the biblical narrative to explore the tradition-oriented Israelite society:

- What story elements contribute to a social interpretation or reconstruction?
- How can significant space be a catalyst in the narrative or an indicator of social values and practices?
- What can a sociological interpretation tell us about the political character of ancient Israel as portrayed in the biblical narrative?
- What can we learn about social institutions in the biblical narrative?

Chapter 5: History and Historiography

What are the sources that contribute to the creation of a history of ancient Israel and Judah?

While topography and climate are major factors in the development of the culture of ancient Israel, an equally decisive factor was the continually evolving political situation between 1200 BCE and 500 BCE. There were a couple of windows of opportunity (1200–900 BCE and 800–750 BCE) during which ancient Israel had the chance to exercise political and economic autonomy. However, it was more often the case that their world was dominated by the political and economic ambitions of the superpowers based in Egypt and Mesopotamia. It would literally be impossible to understand ancient Israel without reference to its contacts with other nations. In fact, much of the theological development and worldview of the ancient Israelites was the direct result of having to cope with military invasions, cultural incursions, and the disastrous realities of quite literally being caught in the middle between these two major civilizations.

The task of this chapter is to provide not only a basic orientation to the history of ancient Israel, as documented in ancient Near Eastern texts and the biblical narrative, but to discuss the writing of their history by the ancient Israelites. Once basic methodological considerations are voiced, I will then present a model for a semiotics of history that will guide our discussion of the source materials available in the writing of a history of ancient Israel. At the same time, I will remind the reader that history and historicity are not always the same thing. It is always difficult to write a completely objective history, and more often than not a history is based on cultural bias or propaganda than fact. To get a taste of this, we will explore the current scholarly dialogue on Israel's history, examining the tools employed by historians and setting out the data that they use to make their case.

In the end, I will ask a series of questions that will center on the use of sources and provide a brief case study to help illustrate how they might be answered:

- What do we really know about the history of ancient Israel?

- Can the biblical account be utilized as a source for writing a history of Israel?
- How do we create a dialogue between a biblical narrative, extrabiblical texts, and archaeological data?

Scope of the Study

Studying the ancient Israelites is always going to be a work in progress. Each of these chapters is designed in its own way and collectively to provide a path to the world of ancient Israel. It has been my experience as a historian and a biblical scholar that one must explore a variety of paths and methods while keeping in mind that these avenues of research are infinite and constantly evolving. As I note in chapter 3 when discussing literary analysis of the textual resources of the ancient Near East, the clues that contribute to our study are like pieces of an ancient mosaic floor. No single tile can provide a sense of the whole image. We must therefore put them together very carefully, testing to see if they fit the pattern. In the end we may then make tentative statements about the artist(s) as well as the social world that contributed to their creative ideas. The process of drawing conclusions is the reward for a careful examination of the data. I hope that this volume will provide my readers with the tools to draw their own educated conclusions about a world that has vanished and yet lives on in its sources and in the echoes that it has produced in our own world.

1

Historical Geography

What do topography, ecology, and climate have to do with shaping the culture and identity of ancient Israel?

Over the years I have discovered that one of the chief roadblocks my students run into is not being able to visualize the physical stage upon which ancient Near Eastern history and biblical events took place. Many of them have not traveled overseas, and those who have generally have not visited the Middle East. This presents an immediate problem for visual learners, who need to see and experience a place for it to truly come alive. It is hard to find your way around a story's physical details if you cannot summon up a mental map to remind you of landmarks and directions. Add to this the sensory overload of strange-sounding geographic names that readers confront in the biblical text, and many simply skip over these details.

As a result, few students are really aware of how ancient cultures and their history are impacted by the terrain in their respective regions. If we think at all about ancient Israel, we often fall back on a stereotypical image of a desert region instead of the multifaceted landscape that actually exists in that region. This lack of familiarity or even empathy for the real conditions that exist outside our own framework of experience is an indication that if one does not live in a particular area, one is less likely to be aware of such things as obstacles to travel, major streams and rivers, interesting scenic vistas, and the shift from one type of topography to another. Furthermore, if one has not experienced life in a Mediterranean climate, the concept of a wet and a dry season rather than the variable patterns of summer, fall, winter, and spring will present some difficulties.

How many of us really think about physical resources like soil conditions, rainfall amounts, and a lack of flat surfaces for farming? If we live in farm country this may be a concern, but for urban dwellers it would seldom if ever come to mind. Marginal areas are even less likely to strike a note of familiarity. After all, when was the last time you concerned yourself with the effects of deforested hillsides, scorched steppe or desert areas, or marshy regions that impede passage or commercial use? These are just foreign concepts for most of us.

While it may not sound exciting to discuss the scenery of stories that include these conditions, it is a truism that the set provides not only the backdrop but also the mood for the play. The trick may be to try to sift through all of the data and still find a way to make it sufficiently inviting to readers so that they can appreciate how historical geography can make the biblical narratives jump off the

---

Bible Atlas

Since a narrative description goes only so far, an important tool to add to your library is a Bible atlas (see list at end of chapter). They come in all price ranges and in electronic versions and will provide the spatial and environmental character of the lands of the Bible. Keep yours handy for quick reference checks and reorientation.

page by highlighting real locales where real events took place. Since a comprehensive literature already provides the geographic details of the ancient Near East (see the atlases listed in the bibliography), I will instead concentrate my efforts here on how historical geography can provide a better understanding of the world of the ancient Israelites. This will, however, require us to pay close and repeated attention to the maps available in textbooks or Bible atlases.

Basics of Historical Geography

To begin our discussion and to demonstrate the value of historical geography, let me start with a brief discussion of its basic features and the tools employed by historical geographers. This scientific approach includes the reconstruction of past geographies (the conception of space or landscape as imagined or described by its inhabitants; Seymour 2000) and the examination of geographical changes through time, especially those that have occurred as a result of human efforts (e.g., irrigation, dams, terracing; Powell 2000). Historical geography also makes use of ancient and more modern travel accounts, and it studies the changes that have taken place in political boundaries, ethnic identities, and the cultural landscape (B. Graham 2000). One particular realm of study involves the influences that geographical conditions have upon the course of history in particular regions (Darby 1962; Newcomb 1969).

The methodological investigations of modern historical-geographical research encompass several areas of study. Like other social scientists, geographers recognize that their data will not be complete and will therefore have its limitations. For instance, they cannot simply use the Bible or other ancient texts as a comprehensive guidebook to the lands of ancient Syria-Palestine. Among the methods that they employ are the following:

- **Comprehensive investigations of a geographical region's topography and climate** examine such things as rainfall patterns, major climatic shifts, seismic activity, and soil erosion throughout the periods of occupation to help determine how these factors influenced cultural development.

- **Archaeological surveys** throughout the region create a grid of settlement patterns over a specific period of time (Miller 1991a). These broad surveys involve traversing and photographing the land (aerial views if possible), taking note of probable settlement sites and ancient highways, taking samples of pottery and other artifactual remains on the surface, and speculating on demographic patterns from antiquity to the present.

- **Regular and salvage archaeological excavations** at both urban and rural sites give attention to how architecture, farming methods, and resource exploitation are influenced by topography and climate. Since archaeology by its nature does not completely excavate sites, it is best to obtain a good cross-section of both urban and rural sites to gain a broader picture of living conditions and cultural achievements within the framework of the requirements of physical geography (something that often sparks technological innovations like irrigation techniques, terracing, and architectural styles).

- **Examination of historical records** is vital. Ancient maps such as the Babylonian clay tablet map (ca. 600 BCE) provide some data, although they also demonstrate the limitations of the ancient worldview. Others, such as the Madaba map (http://198.62.75.1/www1/ofm/fai/FAImap.html), a mosaic embedded in the floor of

St. George's church in Madaba, Jordan, provide architectural detail, ancient city names, and a general sense of geographic orientation, while modern toponyms (city names) help provide references to geographic factors and the locations of ancient cities and towns (Black 1997: 5). As a means of authenticating site locations (e.g., How do we know that Tell es-Sultan is actually Jericho or that

Babylonian clay tablet map (Courtesy of Zev Radovan)

the Palestinian village of Beitun is ancient Bethel?), all available records and maps need to be consulted as well

Madaba (Medeba) map (Courtesy of Jim Yancey)

Factors in Middle Eastern Historical Geography
(adapted from Rubin 1990: 30–33)

Climate   The Mediterranean climate, with its wet winter (October to mid-April) and dry summer (June to September), prevailing west winds coming off the sea, and scorching east winds from the desert—all contribute to the introduction of irrigation systems, thick-walled architecture, seasonal warfare, and a farming economy based on wheat, grapes, and olives. Settlement patterns tend to cluster initially in regions of higher annual rainfall and eventually expand to more mountainous or arid regions due to population, economic, and political pressure.

Topography   The physical terrain of Canaan, with several distinct zones (Coastal Plain, Shephelah Plateau, Central Hill Country, Jordan Valley, Negev Wilderness) in a small total area (60 miles wide by 150 miles long), allows for great variation in settlement patterns—rural, urban, seminomadic, and seasonal. Natural defenses and proximity to trade routes and natural resources are also factors in the placement of cities.

Water sources   The availability of water (rivers, springs, wells, and summer dews) and the technology to store (cisterns, reservoirs) and channel (aqueducts) this vital liquid is a limiting factor in the creation of settlements. There is real meaning to having the rains fall "in their season" (Lev. 26:4). Economic diversity is also influenced by annual rainfall (five inches at Jericho, seventeen inches at Jerusalem, thirty-two inches in Galilee) and elevations (3,200 feet above sea level in Jerusalem to 1,300 feet below sea level at the Dead Sea). Archaeological and current evidence help to determine ancient settlement patterns.

Natural resources   The proximity of natural resources such as mineral deposits, quarries, bitumen, and salt is a determination in settlement patterns.

---

as lingering linguistic traditions that may indicate the survival of a place name.

The findings from these studies are then integrated into a comprehensive report that attempts to describe "the development of the settlement pattern, with all of its components, over an entire region during consecutive historical periods . . . and to analyze the interrelationships between a variety of factors—geographical, cultural, economic and social— that have influenced this development" (Rubin 1990: 28).

▶

This may transcend normal decisions in inaccessible and arid regions based on overriding economic concerns.

Agriculture   Since farming was a primary factor in ancient Israel's economy and a link to survival in the rural settlements of the Central Highlands, archaeological surveys must include identification of the artifactual remains of ancient agriculture (terraces, oil and winepresses) and must study the history of agriculture, its technology, and its innovation. This may be done initially without regard to historical period and simply as an examination of the relics of ancient practice, their function, and their significance.

Demography   Archaeological surveys have mapped the size and distribution of rural and urban population centers, providing data from which to extrapolate population size and density in antiquity. By combining the data on demography, water resources, and levels of agricultural activity, the "bearing capacity" of the land can be determined in combination with evidence of positive (trade, travel) and negative (invasion, warfare) external contact.

Architecture   Examination of architectural remains, including private, cultic, and civic structures, provides insight into urban planning, development of cities and fortifications, foreign influences or innovations, and adaptation to climatic and topographic conditions.

Social structure and cultural identity   Social mechanisms and phenomena (religious practices, introduction of monarchy) affect population, economic development, and settlement patterns. Contact with other cultures can lead to integration of new ideas or negative reactions emphasizing local models or customs as a cultural defense mechanism.

By including an entire region in the study, it is possible to determine the wider ranging environmental, political, and economic factors that are keys to the development of settlement patterns as well as political and economic change (both urban and rural).

Orienting Yourself to the Geography of Ancient Israel

One way to begin an orientation to the geography of ancient Israel is to look for instances in ancient Near Eastern texts, such as the Assyrian royal annals or the biblical text, where the writers or storytellers make explicit references to the dimensions or topography of the region. For example, one commonly repeated phrase that provides a shorthand version of the north-south dimensions of the Promised Land is "from Dan to Beersheba" (Judg. 20:1; 2 Sam. 17:11). This is simply a euphemism for the whole country, from end to end, without being specific about its geographic character or political divisions. In a similar way, the United States celebrates its length and breadth in one of its most familiar songs ("America the Beautiful") using the phrase "from sea to shining sea." A more comprehensive orientation to the way the ancient Israelites viewed their world is found in the description of the division of the land into tribal districts in Joshua 15–21. This account is coupled with the designation of three "cities of refuge," a judicial answer to blood feud, and therefore provides us with some sense of standard travel times and distances between districts (Auld 1978).

While the narrative in which Joshua gathers the tribal elders at Shiloh and allocates their specific portions of the land actually reflects later political boundaries, it does provide a convenient outline of the nation and its various regions (Svensson 1994: 18). Given its nature as a quasi-legal document that functioned as one of the pieces needed to create a spatial identity for each tribe, there is more information here than is necessary for a basic survey of the land. It can be broken down into its major component parts:

- In Joshua 20:7, all of the land of Canaan west of the Jordan River is divided into three regions extending from north to south: (1) Galilee (Hill Country of Naphtali), (2) Hill Country of Ephraim, and (3) Hill Country of Judah. The dimensions of the land are then tied to the locations of the cities of refuge for these regions: Kedesh (seventeen miles northwest of the Sea of Galilee), Shechem (thirty

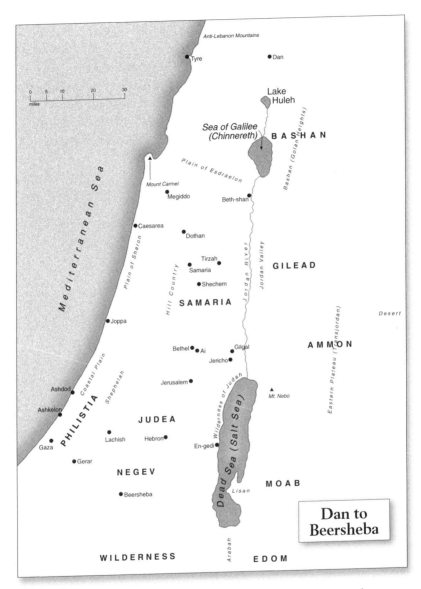

Dan to Beersheba

miles north of Jerusalem), and Hebron (twenty miles southwest of Jerusalem). This is comparable to the "staking out" of the land when Abraham constructed a series of altars at Shechem, Bethel, and Hebron as he traveled south (Gen. 12:7–8; 13:18).

- Joshua 15:1–12 provides four geographic districts within Judah: the Lowlands or valley area, the Mountain, the Negev, and the Wilderness—all with very explicit boundary markers. Given this region's political importance in later periods, it is not surprising to find such specificity and attention to detail.

- Joshua 17:14–18 divides what will become Samaria in the divided monarchy into three regions: the

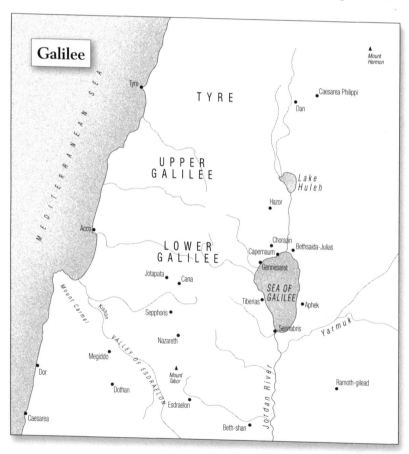

Hill Country, the Plain, and the Forest—all of which correspond to the central portion of the country or the Hill Country of Ephraim. Again, the political importance, as the heart of the northern kingdom of Israel, demands a clear differentiation of its geographic character.

In this way the ancient Israelites were able to visualize their territory as a whole as well as its political and kin-based divisions. Because they were intimately familiar with this area, they did not include a great deal of information on its geographic features beyond its major boundary markers. Of course, some general idea of the topography is contained in designations like "wilderness" or "hill country," and a token reference to its natural resources is found in designations like "the plain" and "the forest." But, after all, they had walked this land and had a mental as well as physical sense of its character. Therefore, what would have been of particular importance in this account to the Israelite audience are the specific details of tribal boundaries. They needed this information in order to create a formal "deed to the Promised Land" that they could point to or recite (see the recitations of "covenant history" in Psalm 78 and Psalm 105) as part of their sense of national identity and ownership.

An idealized conception of the Promised Land is found in the narrative in which Moses goes to the top of Mount Nebo. From this vantage point he is allowed by God to view the Promised Land just prior to the initiation of the conquest. The episode begins with Moses's climb "from the plains of Moab to Mount Nebo, to the top of Pisgah, which is opposite Jericho" (Deut. 34:1). Mount Nebo is located in the southern portion of Gilead in the central Transjordan region, nine miles east of the north end of the Dead Sea, and has an elevation of 2,740 feet. From this height it should be

---

Land Deeds

Having a title to land was a significant achievement for a household in the ancient Near East, and as a result land did not usually pass out of the family without some extraordinary factors coming into play. For instance, in the Nuzi texts (Matthews and Benjamin 2006: 47–49) a legal fiction was created in some cases in which a purchaser was adopted into a household. This also helps explain why the land was an essential element in the covenant promise. A landowner was not only a member of the covenant community, he was also a link in a multi-generational chain extending back to Abraham's time and continuing into the future. As a result many laws and stories include either a mention of land deeds or the protection of property rights within set boundary markers.

Middle Assyrian Law A.45   A soldier who is taken as a prisoner of war may regain his rights to his land and property on his return. The land is reassigned by the king only if word is received that the man has died while in captivity.

Genesis 23:17–18   Abraham purchases the Cave of Machpelah to bury his wife and to serve as a burial site for his family. It is the first documentation of ownership of a portion of the Promised Land by a member of the covenant community.

2 Samuel 24:21–25   David purchases the threshing floor of Araunah the Jebusite to build an altar to thank God at the end of a plague. Solomon later builds the temple on this site (2 Chron. 3:1), which had been consecrated by David and transformed from Jebusite to Israelite property.

Jeremiah 32:6–15   Jeremiah "redeems" his cousin Hanamel's field "at Anathoth in the land of Benjamin" to keep the property in his family.

Kudurru boundary marker

---

possible to look over long distances across the Jordan Valley toward Jericho and well into Canaan.

On a physical level a real difficulty arises when considering this story. The evaporating mist that rises continuously from the Dead Sea tends to obscure visibility when looking to the west into Canaan, but this narrative is not about physical sight.

It also serves as an enacted prophecy demonstrating that even during the final siege of Jerusalem the people can retain hope in an eventual return to the land and the restoration of their legal/covenantal rights.

Boundary Markers

***Kudurru* Boundary Marker**   A Babylonian practice was to record land grants by a king to his vassals with an inscribed stone detailing the stipulations of the grant and calling on the gods to witness and enforce the agreement. The finely carved *kudurru* generally would be stored in a temple, while a clay copy was held in trust by the vassal, and a much rougher stone was actually placed at the boundary of the land.

Egyptian Book of the Dead   One of the "declarations of innocence" uttered by the spirit of the deceased was "I have not moved boundary markers of another's fields" (Matthews and Benjamin 2006: 221).

Genesis 31:43–55   Laban and Jacob establish clear territorial boundaries and rights between their territories (Haran in northern Syria and Canaan) by making a treaty, eating a covenant meal, and setting up a boundary marker (Morrison 1983: 163).

Deuteronomy 19:14   Deep concern is expressed in several legal texts forbidding anyone from moving a neighbor's boundary marker "on the property . . . allotted to you in the land that the LORD your God is giving you to possess." Thus a curse is invoked on anyone who moves a neighbor's boundary marker (Deut. 27:17), and Wisdom literature repeats the maxim: "Do not remove an ancient landmark or encroach on the fields of orphans" (Prov. 23:10).

1 Kings 21:16   Landowners like to step off what is theirs, as Ahab does when he takes possession of Naboth's vineyard. The land was surveyed in triangles with a boundary marker placed at each corner. Since they walked off the land in sandals, their footwear became symbolic of landownership (Deut. 25:5–10) and their title to the land (Matthews and Benjamin 1993: 114).

Instead Moses is assisted by God to create a mental map for later generations in the land of promise (Nelson 2002: 396). This functions as an example of second or "imagined space," allowing God to once again renew the covenant promise of land by sketching out the dimensions of the country that they will inherit (Matthews 2003a: 12). The panoramic view

---

View of the Promised Land

"Look from the place where you are, northward and southward and eastward and westward; for all the land that you see I will give to you and to your offspring forever." (Gen. 13:14–15)

"Go into the hill country of the Amorites as well as into the neighboring regions—the Arabah, the hill country, the Shephelah, the Negeb, and the seacoast—the land of the Canaanites and the Lebanon, as far as the great river, the river Euphrates." (Deut. 1:7)

"Go up to the top of Pisgah and look around you to the west, to the north, to the south, and to the east." (Deut. 3:27)

"Ascend this mountain of the Abarim, Mount Nebo, which is in the land of Moab, across from Jericho, and view the land of Canaan, which I am giving to the Israelites for a possession." (Deut. 32:49)

"The LORD showed him the whole land: Gilead as far as Dan [the northern view], all Naphtali, the land of Ephraim and Manasseh [the view of the central region to the west], all the land of Judah as far as the Western Sea [the view to the southwest], the Negeb, and the Plain . . . as far as Zoar [the view to the south]." (Deut. 34:1–3)

"From the wilderness and the Lebanon as far as the great river, the river Euphrates, all the land of the Hittites, to the Great Sea in the west shall be your territory." (Josh. 1:4)

---

described in Deuteronomy 34:1–3 and other passages spans the regions starting in the north as far as the Euphrates River (Deut. 1:7), extending southward through the central portion of Canaan, traveling through the highlands of Judah, and then panning on down to the Negev and the wilderness.

Familiarity of Place

A close reading of the biblical narrative quickly shows just how small the land of ancient Israel actually was. Very simply, one keeps running into the same place names, due in part to there being only a limited number of significant cities and towns in ancient Israel. Situated at strategic points, they guarded crossroads or took advantage of nearby trade routes. In those few cases where a major settlement appeared off the beaten track, its origin was usually based on the exploitation of a mineral resource or a perennial water source. As time went on, these well-placed population centers grew into cities that housed political leaders, temples, and prosperous merchants. They also served as market hubs for the produce and products of the surrounding villages (called "daughters" in Ezek. 16:46–55). Of course, no city retains its importance throughout its history. While geography might play a role in a city's being founded and may contribute to its rise to prominence, natural disaster (e.g., earthquake in Amos 1:1) or political change may in turn leave it a forgotten, backwater town or an abandoned ruin (Jer. 26:6–9) (Noort 1997: 161–62).

By keeping a running tally of the number of major events that occur in the biblical account at particular places, it is possible to get a sense of the confluence of history, tradition, and geography. It may even have been expected that significant battles, political conferences, prophetic pronouncements, or festivals must take place in those towns that had previously gained notoriety. In other words, familiarity plays a role in the expected setting of a narrative in order to give it or its characters greater authority. God may speak to Moses on a barren hillside in an uninhabited wilderness (Mount Sinai), but thereafter that place takes on a new character that demands that it be the site for future events (e.g., Exod. 24; 32).

Kings will see the value of tying themselves to earlier leaders or victorious generals by staging their coronations or other official acts at the sites of previous triumphs or turning points for the nation. This helps to explain why Saul delayed his acclamation as king by the tribal elders. Instead of staging a celebration at the site of his victory (Jabesh-gilead, north of the Jabbok River and seven miles east of the Jordan River), which was a site without much traditional significance, Saul chose to assemble the elders at Gilgal (one and a half miles northeast of Jericho) inside Canaan (1 Sam. 11:14–15) (Polzin 1988). Here Joshua had initiated the conquest of the Promised Land by crossing the Jordan River (Josh. 4:19–20), and Saul surely hoped to position himself in the minds of the people as the "new Joshua." He therefore chose to begin his reign on the site where the last national leader of the people had led them to victory.

As the conquest narrative in Joshua indicates, the Israelites did not build their nation in an empty land; many of the cities mentioned in the biblical narrative had existed long before the appearance of Israel on the stage of history. For instance, archaeological excavations at Jericho have revealed occupation layers reaching back to approximately 8000 BCE. Jerusalem, which would eventually become Israel's capital city, had, according to the mid-fourteenth-century BCE El Amarna tablets, an earlier incarnation as a Canaanite citadel ruled by an Egyptian political appointee. This prior history of settlement explains in part the inclusion of scribal glosses in the text that provide both old and new names for cities. For instance, Hebron was previously named Kiriath-arba (Josh. 15:13), Dan was originally named Laish (Judg. 18:29), and Jerusalem was known as Jebus (Josh. 18:28).

Another demonstration of the way in which the ancient Israelites could have oriented themselves spatially within a narrative is the episode in Amos 1–2, where this prophet lays out a general condemnation of Israel and all of its immediate neighbors. After his call as a prophet, Amos travels north from his home village of Tekoa, which is located twelve miles southwest of Jerusalem in the Hill Country of Judah, to the neighboring kingdom of Israel. He takes his stand at Bethel (twelve miles north of Jerusalem), one of the cultic centers that had been established by King Jeroboam at the time of the division of the kingdom (1 Kings 12:29–30). Choosing Bethel as the site for his prophetic pronouncements provides Amos with a perfect setting for

Major Cities and Their Traditional Authority

Shechem   The twin peaks of Mount Ebal and Mount Gerizim dominate the city of Shechem in the Central Hill Country (thirty miles north of Jerusalem). Easy access to trade routes going both west and east—the Via Maris and King's Highway—makes this site one of the major crossing points. Its traditional authority is attached to Abraham's entrance to Canaan here (Gen. 12:6–7), Joshua's covenant renewal ceremony following the conquest (Deut. 11:29; Josh. 24), and Rehoboam's disastrous meeting with the tribal elders (1 Kings 12:1–17). Its political importance diminishes with the move of the northern kingdom's capital to Samaria (1 Kings 12:25; 16:24).

Shiloh   Located in the Ephraimite Hill Country between Shechem and Bethel (ten miles north of Bethel and twenty miles northeast of Jerusalem), Shiloh lies just east of the trade route (Judg. 21:19). Its fame rests on the story of Joshua's division of the land (Josh. 18:1), its use as a cultic center where the ark of the covenant resided in Eli's time (1 Sam. 4:3–4), and the reference to its ruins as a sign of God's displeasure (Ps. 78:60; Jer. 7:12–14).

Bethel   Mentioned seventy-one times in the Old Testament (second only to Jerusalem), the city of Bethel is located twelve miles north of Jerusalem on the Ephraim-Benjamin border (Josh. 16:2). It is tied to both Abraham (Gen. 12:8) and Jacob (Gen. 28:19) and is the site of one of King Jeroboam's two shrines (1 Kings 12:32–33). It is a target of the prophet Amos (Amos 5:5–6) and is rebuilt by returning exiles during the Persian period (Ezra 2:28).

Jericho   Situated fifteen miles northwest of Jerusalem near a powerful spring, the city of Jericho lies six miles west of the Jordan River and ten miles northwest of the Dead Sea. A Jordan River ford near the city links it to the trade route from Transjordan into the Judean Hill Country and extending to the coastal highway in the west. In the biblical narrative, it is linked to Joshua's conquest (Josh. 2; 6), the judge Ehud's murder of King Eglon of Moab (Judg. 3:12–30), and Elijah's ascension (2 Kings 2:4–5).

Hebron   Located twenty miles southwest of Jerusalem on the mountain ridge that formed the main north-south route in the Judean Hill Country connecting Jerusalem with Beer-sheba, Hebron has strong ties to Abraham (Gen. 13:18; 23:18). It functions as a Levitical city and city of refuge (Josh. 20:7; 21:11) and serves as David's capital when he ruled the tribe of Judah (2 Sam. 5:5). Abner is murdered and buried here (2 Sam. 3:27–32), and Absalom uses Hebron as his political jumping-off point for his revolt against David (2 Sam. 15:7–10).

Analyzing Amos's Eightfold Oracle against the Nations

Amos 1:3–5 condemns **Aram** (Syria), which is located northeast of Israel, for its incursions into the Israelite territory in Gilead. The Assyrians defeat the Syrian kings ("House of Hazael" and Ben-Hadad), capture Damascus, and exile its people. Reference to Kir may be a literal place of exile or, because it is the original homeland of the Arameans, a metaphorical way of saying that God has sent these enemy peoples back to their beginnings, eliminating all of their former gains in territory, wealth, and prestige. The oracle against Aram includes these places:

- **Damascus**—capital city of Aram (Syria)
- **Gilead**—central Transjordanian region associated with Israel
- **Valley of Aven**—plain between the Lebanon and anti-Lebanon Mountains separating Israel from Syria in the north
- **Beth-eden**—Aramean kingdom in Syria, two hundred miles northeast of Israel
- **Kir**—original homeland of the Arameans, located in either northern Syria or on the border between the Tigris River and Elam (northern Iran) in the east

Amos 1:6–8 condemns **Gaza**, one of the Philistine city-states located on the southern border with Egyptian Sinai, as a collective term for all of Philistia. Three other cities and one kingdom are listed in the indictment as the prophet traces their territory from south to north along the Coastal Plain:

- **Edom**—southernmost Transjordanian kingdom, extending to the Gulf of Aqaba
- **Ashdod**—Philistine city-state
- **Ashkelon**—Philistine city-state
- **Ekron**—Philistine city-state

his diatribes against that city and the nation: "Come to Bethel—and transgress" (Amos 4:4). It also places Amos in direct descent from the unnamed prophet from Judah mentioned in 1 Kings 13, who had condemned King Jeroboam at this shrine on the day when Bethel was officially dedicated (Levin 1995: 309–10).

Since Amos is on foreign soil and is unknown in Bethel, he chooses to stage a street-corner performance designed to attract attention to his message. His strident curses hurled at enemy nations surely would have entertained his enthusiastic audience. However, his finale, condemning Israel, must have frightened them with the seriousness of his charges. What is interesting is Amos's use of a geographic oracle that will literally take his audience full circle, touching on each of their neighbors before zeroing in on them and their sins. His message includes seven oracles against foreign nations (a number associated with completion in the creation accounts). He then adds an eighth oracle against Israel, employing an x + 1 scheme as his dramatic device. This carries his audience beyond simple completion to recognition of their excesses and showcases the full extent of their own covenantal violations (Chisholm 1990; Linville 2000: 407).

As seen in the sidebar, Amos's rhetorical device includes a great deal of detail and lists nations and their major cities. All of these places would have been familiar to his audience, although it is also possible that some of these details were added by later editors to ensure complete coverage of enemy strongholds in their own day. To give a sense of Amos's revolving and all-encompassing condemnations, the graphic below (not drawn to scale), centered on Bethel, serves as a convenient way to visualize the oracle.

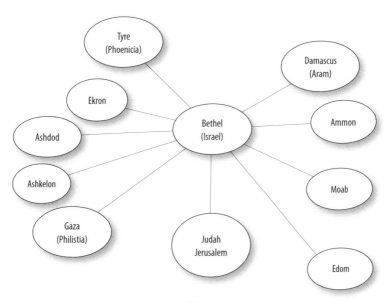

Situating a Story

Looking at the very dense prose found in both Joshua's account of the division of the land and Amos's circular prophecy can be a bit intimidating for most readers. For our purposes, it may be more useful to look at a narrative in the history of the kings of Israel. Before we begin, however, let me point to spatiality theory, which I discuss in more detail in chapter 4. To summarize, space can be divided into "first space" (physical reality), "second space" (imagined space), and "third space" (lived spaced). The majority of our attention in this chapter will be given to physical geography and the environment, that is, the actual places where people live, conduct their business, celebrate their joys, and mourn their sorrows. However, I will also draw on "imagined space" by pointing out in the biblical narrative when certain significant places acquire a meaning that transcends physical reality. For example, Jerusalem, whose location and defensive position in the midst of several hills, served as the political and religious capital of Israel and Judah and is also referred to in portions of the prophetic literature as the "new Eden" (Ezek. 47:1–12; Zech. 14:8) (Matthews 2005: 34).

When the biblical writers mention a geographic site or feature, they are generally describing a place that they and their audience are familiar with. They have walked over each field, climbed the nearby hills, seen the foliage, and smelled the various aromas associated with herding sheep or with cultivating an olive orchard or vineyard. Because their frame of reference is that of a geographic insider, they do not have to go into great detail to conjure up a picture in the minds of their listeners. But these omissions mean that modern readers are often lost amid the strange-sounding place names and are baffled by descriptions of places that are either unknown or so foreign that they cannot even be imagined.

One way to approach the problem of unfamiliar geography in an ancient text is to simply ask the question, "Where are we now?" (Koops 1993). This gives the opportunity to step back a moment and see if anything about the setting of the story looks or sounds familiar. For instance, in the Mesha Inscription composed for the king of Moab in the ninth century BCE, the monarch details an itinerary of his conquests as he drove the Israelites from his territory and expanded his rule into the Madaba-Ataroth-Jahaz area (Na'aman 1997: 85). Since it provides a wealth of information on the cities conquered and regions restored to Moabite control, the inscription provides a general orientation to the area and to the king's military operations (Matthews and Benjamin 2006: 168–69). To explore this in more depth, let us take a biblical narrative and examine the time and space elements that it contains. Our exercise in this case will require careful reading of the text to draw out major plot elements and then will concentrate on geographic issues.

Absalom's Revolt (2 Samuel 15–17)

The series of episodes surrounding Absalom's revolt is part of a larger chronicle sometimes referred to as the Succession Narrative. They describe the origins and details of the struggle between David's sons as they strive to become his successor as the king of Israel (Frolov 2002). Conflict between the brothers, which included the rape of Absalom's sister Tamar (2 Sam. 13:1–22), escalated to the point where Absalom arranged the murder of his brother Amnon (13:23–33) (Matthews and Benjamin 1997). This violent act is a foreshadowing of later events, but initially it leads to a forced exile for Absalom, who flees Jerusalem, going northeast to Geshur in Aram (Syria) for three years (13:37–38). David eventually is convinced by Joab, his chief advisor and general, to allow Absalom to return to Israel's capital city of Jerusalem, but there is no true reconciliation between father and son (14:1–24).

Absalom's Steps to Power

2 Samuel 14:25–27   Absalom's physical beauty "there was no blemish in him" is comparable to the young David, who "was ruddy, and had beautiful eyes, and was handsome" (1 Sam. 16:12). Absalom had also proven his virility by fathering three sons and a daughter.

2 Samuel 14:28–33   After being patient for two years, Absalom sends Joab to David with the message to either return him to the royal court or have him killed. This act of contrition, coupled with his effacing himself before the king's feet (14:33), creates an image of trust and loyalty to David.

2 Samuel 15:1   With an official place once again at court, Absalom gets a chariot and horses (a trapping of power; see Gen. 41:43) and an entourage of fifty men to "run ahead of him" (1 Sam. 8:11; 1 Kings 1:5).

2 Samuel 15:2–6   Absalom takes advantage of the symbolic authority attached to the city gate to station himself there and proclaim that, while David has failed to provide justice to the people, "if only I were judge in the land," then every suit would be given a just hearing. In this way, he "stole the hearts of the people of Israel" (15:6).

In the face of the estrangement with his father, Absalom therefore decides to take matters into his own hands by staging events that will increase his popularity with the people (15:1–6) and by gathering a following among the younger men (Beek 1994). Each step he takes is designed to add the symbolic trappings of power to his public persona and to create among the people the general sentiment that he should be king (Daube 1998: 318–19).

Here is where geography becomes particularly important to the plot of the story. Having already built up his image over a period of four years as a rightful claimant to the throne, Absalom asks permission to go to Hebron to "pay the vow that I have made to the LORD," thanking God for returning him to Jerusalem (2 Sam. 15:7–8). David, who seems to have been oblivious to Absalom's political moves, of course, cannot refuse this request to fulfill a vow made to God. With royal permission granted, Absalom uses the opportunity to gather two hundred men who will accompany him to Hebron and will form the core of his army when he subsequently marches on Jerusalem to take the throne away from David (15:11–12). At this point we should step back and ask two significant questions:

1. Where is Hebron in relation to Jerusalem? Jerusalem is located on two hilly ridges at the southern end of the Benjamin plateau in the Central Hill Country, just off of the major trade routes that run along the spine of the Hill Country. Hebron is located on this mountain ridge twenty miles southwest of Jerusalem on the main north-south route in the Judean Hill Country that connects Jerusalem with Beer-sheba at the southern end of the country. It is strategically placed as a link to the western area of Judah, tying the Hill Country to the Shephelah Plateau and the border town of Lachish. Hebron was also a market center with produce transported here from the surrounding Hill Country as well as from the desert and steppe regions to the south (Rasmussen 1989: 41–42).

2. Why did Absalom ask to go to Hebron? The answer to this question is based on the traditional history of Hebron as the site of the ancestral burial cave of Machpelah (Gen. 23) and on the political history of Hebron as the seat of David's power for seven years after the death of King Saul (2 Sam. 2:1–11). By going there Absalom links himself to the covenantal promise to Abraham and proclaims to his contemporaries that he is David's true successor. Geography therefore plays a significant political role in this story.

Having linked himself politically to David's original power base at Hebron, the rebellious son begins a march north to Jerusalem at a pace slow enough to allow his supporters to join his procession and swell his army to the extent that David will find it necessary to abandon the capital and flee without

41

a fight (2 Sam. 15:13–15). The twenty miles he had to cover were over an established trade route along the ridgetop, and it is easy to envision his army's confident movements, welcoming supporters to their ranks from villages along the way and perhaps even being cheered on by the people.

This episode in the account of David's kingship also brings up the extreme importance of Jerusalem as the political and religious capital of the nation. At the beginning of David's rule, Jerusalem was most likely a small, unfortified town without major economic importance (Finkelstein 2003: 83; Killebrew 2003: 334). Hebron, with its links to major trade routes, was a regional market center and a good choice when David made it his seat of power for over seven years. However, it was located too far south to serve as a national capital for all of the Israelite tribes, and of course it was politically affiliated with the tribe of Judah.

According to the Succession Narrative, after the death of Saul's son Ishbaal (2 Sam. 4), the tribal elders traveled from throughout the country to Hebron in order to offer the leadership of the nation to David (5:1–5). Realizing that this meant he would have to abandon his present capital and choose one more centrally located, David turned his attention to Jerusalem, which had certain advantages that outweighed its less desirable location off the main trade routes. First, its citadel was defended by surrounding hills and deep valleys. It also had a ready water supply in the Gihon Spring, and it possessed a long history of remaining unconquered (Judg. 1:21). This also meant that the city was politically neutral since none of the Israelite tribes had been able to claim it as their own. Once David managed to capture the city (the details are too sketchy to explain how he did it) and install his administration there, he could transform it into his own city. One example of how he accomplished this is his transporting the ark of the covenant, the gold-covered box containing the tablets of the Ten Commandments and representing God's presence among the people, to Jerusalem

(2 Sam. 5:6–12; 6:1–19). In this way, its geographic short-comings were submerged under the veneer of political and religious power (Cahill 2004; Frolov and Orel 1999).

Returning to our narrative of Absalom's revolt, when David's forces were preparing to flee the city, he ordered the Levites who had planned to accompany him to return to the city (2 Sam. 15:24–26). They were transporting the ark of the covenant, but David did not want it to be removed from Jerusalem. The king realized its symbolic importance, and David did not wish to tie it to his political fortunes. To remove an important religious icon from Jerusalem would have diminished its authority and its enduring significance to the nation (Matthews 2004a).

Jordan River (Courtesy of Jim Yancey)

David and those accompanying him then left his hilltop capital, descending the eastern slope of the city into the Kidron Valley and going "up the ascent of the Mount of Olives" dressed as penitents (15:30). After a brief delay to judge Absalom's immediate intentions, the king and his remaining forces crossed the fords of the Jordan River (15:28) and traveled about seven miles east of the Jordan River Valley to Mahanaim near the Jabbok River in the territory of Gilead (17:22–27). Here again an important question of geography arises: Why does David go to Mahanaim? The following list provides some possible answers.

- Mahanaim's location, seven miles east of the Jordan River, protecting the north bank of the ford of the Jabbok River, situates it at a strategic point where it can control the north-south traffic along the major trade route through Transjordan, the King's Highway (see Solomon's appointment of the city as one of his administrative strongholds in 1 Kings 4:14). It is also in close proximity to his Ammonite allies (2 Sam. 17:27–29).
- Ironically, Mahanaim was the administrative center for Saul's son Ishbaal after his father was killed at the Battle of Gilboa (1 Sam. 31:1–7). Ishbaal ruled the northern tribes from this site outside of Canaan for seven years, and it is now reused by David as his seat while in exile from Jerusalem.
- Mahanaim is tied traditionally to the story of Jacob's encounter with "the angels of God" (Gen. 32:1–2) and to his successful meeting with his brother Esau in which the ancestor gained free title to the covenant lands in Canaan (33:1–17). By returning to this traditional site, David may have sought to energize his forces and remind them of his role as king and heir to covenantal leadership.
- Mahanaim is referred to as a Levitical city (Josh. 21:38), and David has a previous history of seeking out Levitical support (see his journey to Nob for Goliath's sword in 1 Sam. 21:1–9).

Given time by the duplicitous counsel of his double agent Hushai (2 Sam. 17:5–14), David will remain in Mahanaim and rebuild his army. Eventually he will return to attack.

His forces will defeat Absalom in the battle of the "forest of Ephraim" (18:6–8). Since both armies have been encamped east of the Jordan in Gilead, this battle scene must have taken place in an area of scrub brush and uneven terrain just south of the Jabbok (McCarter 1984: 405). After spending an inordinate amount of time mourning the death of his traitorous son, David returns to his capital city and is restored to his throne in Jerusalem (2 Sam. 18–19) (Aharoni et al. 1993: 84). The moment when David crosses the Jordan back into Israel (19:11–23) touches a narrative cord since it plays upon two important political traditions: Joshua's crossing the Jordan to begin the conquest of the land (Josh. 3–4) and Saul's acclamation as king over Israel after defeating the Ammonites at Jabesh-gilead (1 Sam. 11). Plus, all of these significant events occur at Gilgal (Joshua in Josh. 4:19–20; Saul in 1 Sam. 11:14–15). When David in turn makes his triumphant crossing and is restored to full authority by the elders (Olyan 1996: 211), this provides a necessary closing of the circle that had been opened by Absalom's revolt and David's flight across the Jordan into exile.

Clearly, this extended narrative plays on the importance attached to Jerusalem, Hebron, and Mahanaim as successive centers of David's power. Once the monarchy was firmly established in Jerusalem during the reign of Solomon, the geographic role of the city expanded to include a wider region. Therefore, the question can now be asked, "Where exactly is Jerusalem in relation to the other nations that are mentioned in the biblical narrative?" To orient yourself in much the same way that one of David's scribes might have done, envision the world from the starting point of Jerusalem, centrally located in the Judean Hill Country just north and west of the Dead Sea. If you were to travel west to the Coastal Plain from Jerusalem, it is only about thirty miles. From there eastward to the Jordan River the distance is only twenty miles.

Looking to the north are the territories occupied by the northern tribes, including the major Israelite cities of Bethel,

Area to the north of Jerusalem (Courtesy of Chris Miller)

Shiloh, Shechem, and Dan (a total distance from Jerusalem of about one hundred miles). Intersecting this region east-west is the Jezreel Valley, with the cities of Megiddo and Beth-shan guarding its entrances, and going further north is the Galilee region and the mountains of Lebanon that separate the country from Phoenicia. Also looking to the north and east is Syria. Syria's capital, Damascus, is only about 135 miles northeast of Jerusalem.

Area to the east of Jerusalem (Courtesy of Jim Yancey)

Directly east of Jerusalem is the Jordan Valley and then the Transjordanian Plateau, with the neighboring kingdoms of Ammon, Moab, and Edom. This area just across the Jordan River also contains two small regions (Bashan and Gilead) that are tied to the Israelite tribes of Manasseh, Reuben, and Gad. They serve as a border with the Transjordanian kingdoms and the aggressive nation of Aram (Syria).

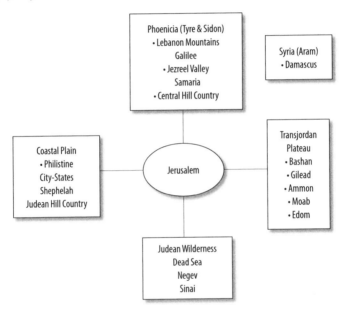

To the south lies the most inhospitable areas of Judah, especially in the arid zone that comprises the area around the Dead Sea and the Judean Wilderness. Further south are the parched Negev steppe region and the Sinai Desert, marking the domain of the nomadic pastoralist and a metaphor for death and suffering (Isa. 27:10; Hos. 2:3). And, finally, to the west are the most fertile and politically hostile areas. Here is the Coastal Plain that gradually rises into the Shephelah Plateau and the Judean Hill Country. It was occupied in David's time by the Philistine city-states and later will be controlled by the superpowers from Egypt or Mesopotamia (Assyria or Babylonia), who take advantage of its rich farm lands and prosperous olive oil industry.

Getting from Here to There: Ancient Trade Routes

In our world of superhighways linking major cities and air transport that can literally take you anywhere on earth in a day, it is hard to imagine what travel must have been like in ancient times. Travel between and within the various regions of the ancient Near East and the eastern Mediterranean often required political cooperation and patience (2 Kings 5:1–8). For security reasons, merchants who were transporting goods to other countries or even within their own country generally traveled only during the daylight hours, although in summer the heat required them to wait until nightfall to begin their journey (Astour 1995: 1402). In Mesopotamia and Egypt, barges traveled along the rivers, but that was not possible along many stretches of the much shallower Jordan River in Canaan. Overland journeys were generally on foot, although donkeys are mentioned as both pack animals and a means of transport for both men (Gen. 22:3; Num. 22:21) and women (Josh. 15:18). Typical distances traveled in a day, depending on the difficulty of the terrain and the weather, averaged around twenty miles, although official couriers on foot (2 Sam. 18:19–23) or mounted would have covered greater distances (Dorsey 1991: 12–13). This means that a journey from Hebron to Jerusalem would ordinarily take one full day, while one from Shechem south to Jerusalem would take a day and a half to cover the thirty miles between them.

Distance and terrain were not the only obstacles to travel in ancient Israel. The countryside was crisscrossed with dry streambeds known as wadis, and in some cases these had cut

The Levite and His Concubine

A good sense of these distances and some of the considerations while traveling are found in the story of the Levite in Judges 19:1–15. He had left "remote parts of the hill country of Ephraim" to journey to his father-in-law's house in Bethlehem (presumably at least a thirty- or forty-mile trip). On the day of his return he was delayed in departing until late afternoon and as a result could not travel very far before evening fell. He had a choice to spend the night at Jebus (five miles from Bethlehem) or journey on a short distance to Gibeah, three miles north of Jebus. Because at that time Jebus was still a Canaanite city, he chose to continue on to Gibeah, where he felt more secure in stopping for the night with his concubine, servants, and donkeys. While this did not turn out to be a good choice for his group, the story does provide a glimpse of travel on personal business.

deep channels that impeded travelers' progress and could require long detours (e.g., Wadi Suweinet dividing Geba and Mishmash in 1 Sam. 14:4–5). Of course, a wadi could also be used as a roadbed. A good example is the Wadi Qelt, which was one of the main routes between Jericho and Jerusalem (fifteen miles apart) during the Iron Age and became a pilgrim highway in the nineteenth century CE (Dorsey 1991: 205). Wagons and carts helped farmers transport their grain from the fields to the threshing floor and on to market (Amos 2:13) and served as conveyances for sacred objects (2 Sam. 6:3) and offerings being brought to shrines (Num. 7:3). When streams and rivers contained rushing water, a traveler had to either swim across (Judg. 3:28; 2 Sam. 17:22) (Beitzel 1985: 40) or seek out a ford. The biblical account mentions several fords, and these must have been well-known places (Judg. 12:5–6; Isa. 16:2).

River traffic is not mentioned in the biblical text, but it was one of the principal means of transporting goods and people in both Egypt, along the Nile, and in Mesopotamia, on both the Tigris and Euphrates Rivers (Dalley 1984: 168–71). A network of canals allowed for transport of agricultural products and helped to irrigate the fields (Exod. 7:19; Ps. 137:1) (T. James 1984: 112). On a larger scale, trade ships

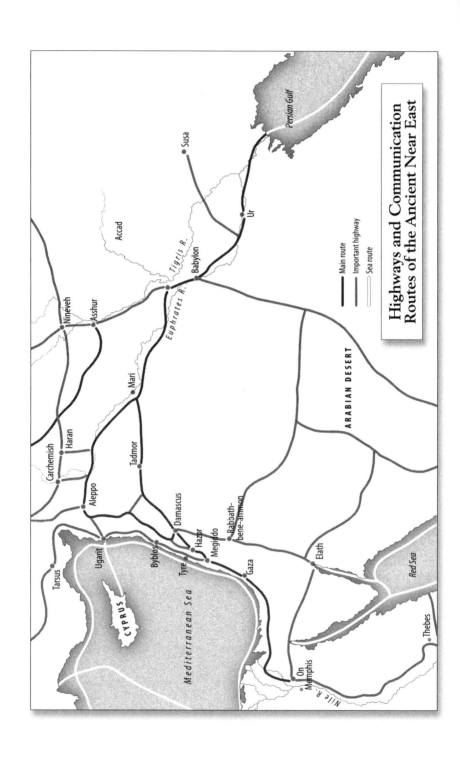

Highways and Communication Routes of the Ancient Near East

plied the waters of the Persian Gulf and the Indian Ocean, to Cyprus and along the Mediterranean, and around the Arabian and Sinai Peninsulas and up the Red Sea to Egypt (1 Kings 9:26–28), generally hugging the coasts or island-hopping (Stieglitz 1984; Artzy 1998). Evidence for such far-flung travel can be seen in the number of shipwrecks being discovered by archaeologists (Linder 1992) and in the list of luxury items and manufactured goods found in Mesopotamian and Egyptian records and in the speeches of the biblical prophets (Ezek. 27).

Overland trade routes also followed the coasts, where the seaports of Phoenicia (Tyre and Sidon) could take raw materials and grain to other markets. In Syria-Palestine, two highways linked Mesopotamia to the Palestinian coast and on to Egypt: the Via Maris and its extension, the Way of the Philistines (Exod. 13:17) along the Sinai-Mediterranean coast, and the King's Highway (Num. 20:17–19), which extended from Palmyra to Damascus and south through Transjordan to the Gulf of Aqabah. Caravan routes along the coast of Arabia from oases like Tema (Job 6:18–19) and up the eastern coast of Africa brought spices, dyes, ivory, incense, and other exotic goods from Africa and India.

Orientation to the Wider Ancient Near Eastern World

With travel as our transition to a wider world, I now want to complete our discussion of historical geography with a general orientation to the far-flung nations of Egypt and Mesopotamia. Standard atlases provide the basic information about these two arid regions, which are ecologically dominated and given life by major river systems (the Nile in Egypt and the Tigris and Euphrates Rivers in Mesopotamia). Without the rivers, organized life could not have existed in these areas. Taking advantage of a reliable water and transportation source, each fostered by 3500 BCE an advanced

Israelite View of Mesopotamia and Egypt

The biblical narrative contains many references to the people's Mesopotamian origins:

Genesis 24:2–4 Desiring to maintain cultural continuity, Abraham forces his servant to take an oath to return "to my country and to my kindred" to obtain a wife for Isaac.

Genesis 31:52 The cultural umbilical cord is cut when Jacob makes a covenant with Laban, marked by a heap of stone, stating "I will not pass beyond this heap to you, and you will not pass beyond this heap and this pillar to me, for harm."

Joshua 24:14–15 At the end of the conquest of Canaan, Joshua cautions the people not to return to "the gods that your ancestors served beyond the River."

Psalm 137:1–6 Mesopotamia is viewed as a land of captivity where the people weep "by the rivers [canals] of Babylon" and swear never to forget their allegiance to Jerusalem.

Egypt serves as a point of origin for the nation based on God's saving act—releasing the Israelites from Egyptian slavery—and provides a strong argument for obedience to the covenant:

Exodus 20:2 The Ten Commandments begin with the reminder that God had brought the Israelites "out of the land of Egypt, out of the house of slavery."

Leviticus 18:3 The postexilic Holiness Code forbids the Israelites to "do as they do in the land of Egypt, where you lived" or "to do as they do in the land of Canaan."

Deuteronomy 4:20 God's actions are designed to shape Israel: "The LORD has taken you and brought you out of the iron-smelter, out of Egypt, to become a people of his very own possession."

Hosea 8:13 Ironically, in the final days of the northern kingdom's existence, just prior to its destruction by the Assyrians, many refugees "return to Egypt" seeing a land that had once been the "house of slavery" transformed for these exiles into a political sanctuary (Wolff 1974: 145–46).

civilization that developed writing and complex political systems. Their polytheistic religious systems reflected the environmental razor's edge in which they lived. Interaction between the two areas was limited in their early history due to the distances involved (over a thousand miles by land). However, both will have a major impact on the world presented in the biblical narrative.

Rather than recite topographic details that can be obtained from reference works, it is more important to highlight how these two centers of ancient civilization are linked to the worldview of ancient Israel. Strong traditional, historical, and cultural influences shaped the intellectual and religious character of the Israelites. Chief among these traditions are the migration of Abram and his family from northern Mesopotamia to Canaan (Gen. 12:4–6) and the exodus after four hundred years of slavery in Egypt (Exod. 12:37–42).

In the realm of superpower politics, Egypt and Mesopotamia (Babylon and Assyria) represent two poles of political ambition. Throughout their history these aggressive nations wished to control the land bridge between them where Israel was located (Matthews 2002a: 70–93). As a result, Syria-Palestine became a frequent battleground where the superpowers could test each other's military and diplomatic resolve. For instance, when the Assyrians besieged Jerusalem in 701 BCE, an Assyrian ambassador stood outside the walls of the city and spoke to Hezekiah's advisors. Among his taunting remarks was the warning that Judah could not trust its alliance with Egypt. They would be wounded by that "broken reed of a staff, which will pierce the hand of anyone who leans on it" (Isa. 36:6). A hundred years later, King Josiah attempted to delay the advance of the Egyptian army as it marched to the aid of its Assyrian allies, and he was killed at the Battle of Megiddo in 609 BCE (2 Kings 23:29).

Viewing the World from a National Perspective

It is only natural that once a nation looks beyond its own borders and immediate neighbors, it tends to orient itself in relation to the ends of the earth, using geographic euphemisms. Thus for the peoples of the ancient Near East, their world included every land "from the rising of the sun to its setting" (Mal. 1:11). The horizons represented the limits of human habitation. The Egyptian "Hymn to the Aten" proclaims that "rays [of the sun rising in the east] enrich the land," while the setting of the sun on the western horizon brought sleep to the land and served as the realm of the gods and the blessed departed (Matthews and Benjamin 2006: 276). At least one view of the Mesopotamian worldview is graphically depicted on a first-millennium map that pictures the earth floating on the waters of the underworld and surrounded by high mountains that served as supports for the heavens (Glassner 1995: 1820). The kings of Assyria expressed their understanding of this worldview by claiming control over as much territory as possible, euphemistically expressed by erecting a monument or stele on the shores of the "Great Sea" or referring to themselves as "king of all the four rims of the earth" (Pritchard 1969: 274–75).

For the Israelites the boundaries of their political control in the north and south are most often expressed by referring to the major rivers in Egypt and Mesopotamia. This explains how Isaiah, in the eighth century BCE, can identify the coming threat represented by Egypt as "the fly that is at the sources of the streams of Egypt" and by Assyria as "the bee" and "a razor hired beyond the River" (Isa.

Israelite Geographic Euphemisms

Psalm 72:8–11 The flowing court language in this coronation psalm heaps blessings and prayers on the new king, endowing him with "dominion from sea to sea, and from the River to the ends of the earth" (repeated in Zech. 9:10).

Jonah 1:3 When Jonah booked passage on a ship to Tarshish in Spain he was literally planning to travel west to the very edge of the known world.

Micah 7:12 In a prophecy of restoration, Micah describes how the people of all nations will come to Jerusalem "from Assyria to Egypt, and from Egypt to the River, from sea to sea and from mountain to mountain."

Zephaniah 3:9–10 In an oracle of transformation, the prophet predicts a reversal of the Tower of Babel division of speech (Gen. 11:1–9), with all peoples speaking a "pure speech" honoring God and bringing offerings from the southernmost reaches of the earth, "from beyond the rivers of Ethiopia."

7:18–20). This sense of boundaries continues down through the Persian period (fifth century BCE), with Ezra referring to Syria-Palestine as "the people of the province Beyond the River" (Ezra 4:10–11).

Of course, there are less idealized descriptions of geography in ancient Near Eastern texts and the Bible. Many citations in official and economic documents note the location of cities, rivers, forests, and trade routes. After all, they knew their world at least as well as we know ours. One sign that these nations clearly understood the basic orientation of their homeland to other countries and regions can be found in their triumphal lists of conquered cities and peoples. For instance, Pharaoh Shishak records the itinerary of his invasion of Syria-Palestine in the late tenth century in which he lists 154 captured towns (Clancy 1999; Redford 1992: 312; compare 1 Kings 14:26). Some of this information can be discounted based on the tendency to boast and to inflate these lists with information from previous campaign inscriptions, but it does provide an interesting link to how invasions were conducted in ancient times.

When we move away from the mundane geographic references and into the realm of song and prophetic speech, it is possible to find major features like the regular inundation of the Nile River being used to enhance a point or to provide a poetic image. Amos (9:5), whose book is dated to an earthquake about 760 BCE, uses the rise and fall of the Nile as a simile for God's control over the destructive power of the earthquake in punishing Israel (Stuart 1987: 393). The life-giving silt that the Nile flood brings to Egypt's fields becomes a metaphor in Jeremiah 46:7–8 for Egypt's desire to "cover the earth" with its armies and "destroy cities and their inhabitants." Jeremiah then proclaims to Egypt's major cities (Migdol, Memphis, Tahpanhes) that their ambitions will be crushed at God's command by Babylonia—"a people from the north" (46:13–24). That assessment of the political situation is reinforced by the account in 2 Kings 24:7

that the king of Babylon had pushed the Egyptians out of Syria-Palestine and "taken over all that belonged to the king of Egypt from the Wadi of Egypt to the River Euphrates" (i.e., Wadi el-Arish in northern Sinai, which flows into the Mediterranean southwest of Gaza).

Final Thoughts

Real and imagined geographies are created to form a world-view by the people of the ancient Near East. Their detailed familiarity with the physical design of their immediate area was necessary to their survival. They had to know where the best soil could be found to plant their crops. They had to know the paths through the hills or along the ridgetops that allowed them easy access to neighboring areas and promoted trade and social interaction. They had to know the resources available in the midst of the major geographic features of their land in order to draw upon them for metals, minerals, and water sources. They had to know the signs of the seasons, the likely shifts in the wind that brought rain or sweltering heat. All these things formed the world in which they lived their lives.

However, an outside world also existed, and for the ancient Israelites this outside world became increasingly important. Located between two superpowers on a land bridge that could not be bypassed because of the desert or the sea, Syria-Palestine was shaped in the crucible of foreign political ambitions and seldom had long periods of peace or isolation. Its historical geography is therefore marked by its topography, its location in relation to other nations, and its creation of a land-based identity as a covenant community.

Bible Atlases

Aharoni, Yohanan, Michael Avi-Yonah, Anson F. Rainey, and Ze'ev Safrai. 1993. *The Macmillan Bible Atlas*. 3rd ed. New York: Macmillan.

Beitzel, Barry J. 1985. *The Moody Atlas of Bible Lands*. Chicago: Moody.

Bimson, John J., and J. P. Kane. 1985. *The New Bible Atlas*. Leicester: Inter-Varsity.

Braybrooke, Marcus, and James Harpur, eds. 1999. *Collegeville Bible Atlas*. Collegeville, MN: Liturgical Press.

Brisco, Thomas C. 1999. *Holman Bible Atlas: A Complete Guide to the Expansive Geography of Biblical History*. Nashville: Broadman & Holman.

Lawrence, Paul, Alan Millard, John Walton, and Heinrich von Siebenthal. 2006. *The IVP Atlas of Bible History*. Downers Grove, IL: IVP Academic.

May, John. 1985. *Oxford Bible Atlas*. New York: Oxford University Press.

Patterson, H. J., Donald J. Wiseman, and John J. Bimson. 1994. *New Bible Atlas*. Downers Grove, IL: InterVarsity.

Pfeiffer, Charles F., E. Leslie Carlson, and Martin H. Scharlemann. 2003. *Baker's Bible Atlas*. Grand Rapids: Baker Academic.

Pritchard, James B. 1997. *HarperCollins Concise Atlas of the Bible*. San Francisco: Harper-Collins.

Rainey, Anson F., and R. Steven Notley. 2006. *The Sacred Bridge: Carta's Atlas of the Biblical World*. Jerusalem: Carta.

Rasmussen, Carl G. 1989. *Zondervan NIV Atlas of the Bible*. Grand Rapids: Zondervan.

Rogerson, John. 1985. *Atlas of the Bible*. New York: Facts on File.

2

Archaeology

How does archaeology contribute to the study of the ancient Israelites?

In the first chapter, I discussed the ways in which historical geography allows scholars and students to better place themselves into the world of the ancient Israelites. In this chapter, I want to dialogue with archaeological data and what it can tell us about the period of history associated with the origins of the Israelite people. Like historians or biblical scholars addressing an ancient text, archaeologists plan their excavations of ancient sites by first doing basic research on the cultural environment of the region and then formulating questions that they hope to have answered or tested during the excavation process. And like other scholars assessing the findings of their research, archaeologists come to understand that the archaeological record that they uncover and observe "consists of nothing more than what we are able to observe at particular stages in our careers . . . and within the limits of our own imaginations" (Bradley 1997: 71). With these limitations in mind it can be shown how artifactual and textual evidence work together to help an archaeologist reconstruct an ancient culture.

In the course of this chapter I will focus on how archaeology is the study of ancient artifacts, whether they be material (e.g., ceramics) or textual (e.g., the Bible) remains. Since this volume is geared to the study of the ancient Israelites, I will place greatest emphasis on the artifactual remains of that culture, including the biblical text. Some people are under the impression that archaeology can be used to prove the biblical account. It cannot do this. The reality is that archaeology has very real limitations, chief of which is the destructive nature of time, the elements, and successive inhabitants of the region who systematically reused building materials and dug pits through ancient occupation layers. It is not unusual for an archaeologist to be systematically and carefully removing layers of soil within a measured square and suddenly discover a plastic drink container mixed in with Roman or Iron Age pottery. While real evidence illuminates the material culture of the peoples who once inhabited ancient Canaan, Philistia, Transjordan, Phoenicia, and Syria, a complete picture is not possible, and conjecture often is more typical of archaeologists than hard and fast conclusions.

In order to make this somewhat clearer, we must understand the theoretical basis for using archaeology to interpret the world of the ancient Israelites and the biblical text. The discussion is not exhaustive, but it indicates the real limitations we face and provides a warning about some of the pitfalls of a too subjective or agenda-driven interpretation of the data.

Excavation Basics—Modern Methods and Allied Sciences

In order to explain the values and limitations of archaeology to the interpretation and evaluation of the cultures of the ancient Near East, I intend to provide a basic description of

Archaeology and Interpretation
(adapted from Davis 2004: 26–28)

1. Once an excavation has begun, the findings may not accord with what we consider to be logical and may require continual reinterpretation. Only the ancients could truly understand the logic of their material remains.

2. It is inappropriate to assign a function or meaning to an artifact or site just because we think it is likely or stands to reason. Since we excavate "the remains of individuals," we must accept that not every artifact makes sense in its context. Some are unique or have an unknown history that we will never fully understand.

3. Since archaeology is a destructive science and nonrepeatable, we must accept the limitations inherent to our current scientific methods and our own record keeping. Many times new interpretations of old data have resulted from the application of new scientific techniques or the reexamination of old published reports.

4. As we excavate we communicate with the material remains of ancient people. This is not a monologue in which the plan for excavation must be slavishly followed no matter what is discovered. Instead it is a continuous dialogue in which we interact, starting with a plan and a set of questions but changing it and them to meet the realities of what is actually discovered. If we seek to find only what we expect, then that is all that we will find.

5. Although archaeologists lay out excavation grids and dig square holes in order to determine stratigraphy and control the flow of data, we must understand that the ancients did not limit their occupation to these fifteen-meter squares. By design and due to the realities of financing fieldwork, no site is completely excavated, and in most cases only about 10 to 15 percent is ever uncovered and analyzed.

6. Since ancient Israelite culture was complex, we cannot expect to answer queries about its nature by asking only simple questions. We must accept that additional data will poke holes in theories that do not take into account the variety of human experience within an equally complex social and physical environment.

7. It is inappropriate to try to force the biblical narrative to conform to an archaeological model, and it is equally inappropriate to limit archaeological investigation so that it is forced to conform to the biblical narrative.

modern excavation techniques and the artifactual evidence produced by fieldwork. Central to this discussion will be the statement that archaeology is neither intended nor able to prove the biblical narrative to be correct. It deals first with the remains of material culture and secondarily with the potential for reconstruction of individual and social behavior (Dever 1998: 232). While these physical objects appear to be only mute testimony to the activities of the ancients, they can be read and reflectively "listened to" in the sense that they serve, in much the same way as the biblical text, as artifacts of the culture that produced them (Dever 1997). Some artifacts, in fact, by their nature suggest how they were used, while others defy immediate interpretation and require the archaeologist to broaden his or her approach to include iconographic or textual sources as reference points (Laato 2005: 170).

To begin our study then, it should be understood that no archaeologist ever goes into the field and blindly thrusts his or her shovel into the earth expecting to shout "Eureka!" when an ancient city or village is miraculously discovered. Instead, careful research goes into determining where to dig. Of course, it is also necessary to obtain a license to excavate and the cooperation of the national agencies involved with conducting archaeological investigations and the preservation of cultural heritage. In most cases today, the licensing procedure also includes a contract that specifies that findings will be presented and published within a set period of time so that the data will not be lost due to inaction or the death of the principal excavator.

Artifacts and Interpretation

The first time I participated in a season of excavation, I worked at the site of Banias (ancient Caesarea Philippi). This is a large city with occupation levels beginning in the

---

Before You Dig

1. **Examine all available ancient records**, including the biblical text, the writings of Greek and Roman historians and travelers, and the chronicles of eighteenth- and nineteenth-century explorers who traveled the ground and in many cases matched modern Arabic names to the ruined mounds, or tells, that dot the landscape of the countries of the Levant. This may allow for a preliminary determination of the identity of the site.

2. **Conduct a survey of the site**, walking about and looking for surface remains such as pottery, architectural features, and a general sense of its size and natural resources. It is important to obtain a clear idea of why a settlement may have been built here even though climate change, erosion, or later construction may have altered or obscured some of these factors.

3. **Use GIS and ground-based sonar** to fix the exact location of the site and determine some understanding of its extent and its hidden features. Since funds and time are limited, it is best to start digging where the visual and the scientific findings indicate the likelihood of uncovering significant architectural or artifactual remains is greatest.

4. **Put together a team** whose expertise will allow for on-site analysis and the preservation of as much data as possible. Optimally, this means that, in addition to the archaeologist and field supervisors and their teams of workers, the site should have the services of an architect, a ceramics specialist, a biologist familiar with the flora and fauna of the region and capable of gathering carbonized as well as microscopic samples, a zoologist to examine and catalog skeletal remains, a geologist who can identify stratigraphic features as well as climatic and geologic change, and an epigrapher, who can read and authenticate inscriptional discoveries.

5. **Establish a plan for each season of excavation** knowing what questions you wish to explore during the systematic opening of portions of the site. Of course, the plan should be flexible enough to take into account new, unexpected data.

Hellenistic period and extending to a modern Arab village that was evacuated during the 1967 Arab-Israeli conflict. It has subsequently become part of a national park, and while we worked in our carefully sketched-out squares, tourists would stop to stare at us and occasionally ask a question about what we were finding. They could see the remains of architectural features but for the most part could not establish a clear pattern because the stratigraphy of the site was fairly complex and there had been a great deal of recycling of building materials in later structures. For instance, the fifth-century CE Byzantine Christian church that dominated one area near the parking lot had large pieces of first- and second-century CE finely carved stones embedded into its foundation and several huge column drums laid on their side as makeshift buttresses for the multistory building.

Students on an archaeological dig (Courtesy of Victor H. Matthews)

Of course, what the tourists really wanted to know was if we had found anything "interesting" that they could photograph and tell their friends about. The magic of archaeology for most people, including student volunteers on their first dig, is the idea of finding and handling something both ancient and significant. For instance, when our group arrived at the site on the first day of the dig, we entered a work shed where the tools were stored and where finds were washed and catalogued. Near the door was a huge pile of pottery sherds. After being told that this was a dump for unwanted pottery, many of the students quickly picked up a few for their own collection. Gradually, these pieces of pottery found their way back to the dump when the students realized (1) how heavy their suitcases were getting and (2) that there was a reason these sherds were being discarded. In the lectures that described the results of each day's excavations, they learned that only complete pots or "diagnostic" sherds indicative of distinctive pottery types, decoration, and style were kept for later study and display. Given the centuries of occupation and the continuous production of new items to replace what had been broken or become outdated, there was simply too great a wealth of cultural debris to save it all. According to set procedure, every sherd was washed and examined to make sure it did not contain an inscription, but the majority was then consigned to the discard pile.

What immediately comes to mind is the sense of frustration attached to trying to find a needle in the haystack. With tons of soil, stones, smashed pottery, ash, and other evidence of occupation and destruction to sort through, it sometimes seems amazing that a picture of the history of a site can be reconstructed at all. To make this somewhat simpler and thus open to informed interpretation, let us begin with the steps associated with a typical archaeological dig in Israel, Jordan, or Syria.

1. Once a site has been located, the necessary permits obtained, and funds raised, then an excavation team is organized. It includes the director, area supervisors, square supervisors, and volunteers; it seldom operates as a democracy. The services of an architect and various scientific experts should be obtained, and if possible they should visit the site and examine the material remains. There will also be a person in charge of preparing and recording the daily finds. The team will usually be housed in a nearby village or hotel and meal service arranged.

2. Since an excavation plan will have already been prepared by the director and senior staff, the first step is to clear the site of the vegetation that has grown since the last season. This procedure facilitates photography, makes surface features stand out, and gets the team used to working together in a sometimes difficult climate.

3. Ten- or fifteen-meter squares are laid out with string and sandbags, and initial levels are taken so that the supervisors will know starting and ending points for each day's work and can determine the exact depth at which significant finds are made.

4. Excavation begins by breaking the soil with shovels and picks, but this may quickly turn to finer work using brushes, ice picks, and trowels when an artifact is discovered or a floor is found, signaling the emergence of a change in stratigraphy. Each day's excavation will end with a careful cleaning and brushing of the square, setting up the next day's work and facilitating early morning photography when the light is best.

5. All pottery and other artifacts are placed in tagged buckets or boxes for later examination. The tags indicate which square and at what level they were found. The recording process in the field will be systematized in later field reports by the square and area supervisors. Unusual finds are also photographed *in situ* to establish a clear provenance and provide as much data as possible for later interpretation.

6. In order to double-check for small finds such as coins, soil removed from a square is sifted through fine-mesh screens or water-filtration processes. This latter technique also aids in recovering carbonized remains of grain and seeds.

7. All tagged buckets and boxes are taken to the collection supervisor for washing or cleaning with an eye

for inscriptions or diagnostic examples that will help establish a ceramic chronology of the site and indicate possible trading activity and, in the case of coins, a clear date for a particular stratum or building.

8. Staff meetings each day go over current findings and formulate new questions that will be addressed in the days to come.

9. At the end of the excavation season, the entire staff completes and submits their field notebooks, and the senior staff spends the next several months analyzing this data while the artifacts are sent to laboratories for scientific tests and classification.

10. Publication of the season's findings should follow as quickly as possible, and a final report of the excavation of the site over a series of seasons should appear in a timely manner for the benefit of the scholarly community.

With these basic steps in the excavation process in mind, we can now turn to the types of artifacts that will form the basis of our interpretation and reconstruction of the social world of the site under study. Each of these items or categories functions as a piece of the puzzle, but because we do not have all the parts only a partial picture will emerge. The artifacts represent a continuum that reaches into the past when a person envisioned the need for an object (a blade to harvest grain, a terraced hillside, a newly shaped lamp), found the means to create it themselves or had someone more skilled do it, put the object into use, and ultimately left it for us to find and speculate on. That thread from invention or innovation, if the object is based on an earlier idea and is simply borrowed, to discovery and analysis allows the archaeologist, like the biblical scholar reading a story, the opportunity to reach back to the emic (i.e., insider) character of the artifact.

Ceramics

In the village culture of ancient Israel many households made their own pottery, but major urban centers relied for their larger needs on specialists who produced mass quantities on a potter's wheel (see Jeremiah's description of the Jerusalem potter at work in Jer. 18:2–4). The result is, of course, that pottery has become the most common artifact found in Middle Eastern excavations. This makes sense because ceramics had to be continually produced to replace broken or damaged ware or to create new styles based on evolving local tastes or imported examples. But ancient pottery designs did not change as often as modern fashions. The cultural conservatism typical of the isolated highland villages of Iron Age I Israel would have placed a barrier on ready acceptance of influences from the more hierarchical, urban-based cultures in the Philistine cities or in Egypt. Larger settlements that had regular contact with foreign merchants may have also been resistant to the adoption of foreign styles and decoration, seeing them as a threat to their cultural identity. In most cases, innovations in pottery design are determined

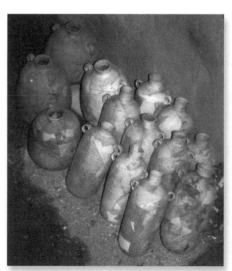

by the principles of relative advantage over existing types and compatibility to specific function. Radical changes or the introduction of new pottery types generally reflect increases in trade, adoption of foreign styles based on conquest, or the appearance of new peoples in an area.

Some styles, for instance those of oil lamps, lasted

Ceramic pottery/artifacts (Courtesy of Jim Yancey)

for decades, and in most cases the basic shapes and functions remained the same for centuries. Because of this, it was possible for nineteenth- and twentieth-century archaeologists to create an initial ceramic chronology based on shapes, styles, and the manner of manufacture and design favored by people in particular places at particular time periods. A good analogy for how archaeologists use this data is the examining of old photographs and dating them to a certain era based on "the clothing, hairstyle, furniture, radios, and even the types of poses assumed by the people in" them (Zevit 2002: 21). Like these modern objects, ancient ones fit into a variety of social and temporal contexts depending on how "up to date" their owners might be. Thus a particular type of pot might exist in a village context longer than in an urban setting less threatened or concerned over changes in style.

Developing a Ceramic Chronology
(adapted from Zevit 2002)

Archaeologists use a variety of means to develop a ceramic chronology that helps to date particular strata associated with the major time periods in ancient Near Eastern history:

1. Basic features of size, design, decoration, and technology of manufacture.
2. Connections between Palestinian pottery and datable events in Mesopotamian or Egyptian history—for instance, by establishing the date of the Assyrian destruction of Lachish in 701 from the annals of the Assyrian kings, the pottery that is found in the destruction level from that event can be dated to that time period.
3. Coordinating the carbon 14 dating of organic materials with the ceramics uncovered in the same excavation levels may assist with the dating of the pottery.

The difficulty with these methods, however, is that pottery vessels may have been produced well before a datable event or before the organic materials were stored in them. Carbon 14 also produces a range of probable dating plus or minus forty years. Thus a pot might be dated within a range of eighty years. This can raise havoc with historians and archaeologists who wish to pinpoint their ceramic chronology and tie that to the beginning or end of a particular era in Israelite or Near Eastern history.

While it may seem that the determination of a relative ceramic chronology for each of the identified historical periods associated with ancient Israel and its neighbors is fairly straightforward, there have been adjustments and controversies over "high" and "low" chronologies. To a certain degree, these scholarly arguments have been based on the percentage of a particular pottery type or decorative element found at ancient sites. It has even hinged on the lack of evidence for a pottery type. Overeagerness to establish a theory or to prove a connection with a biblical event or story can sometimes lead to hasty decisions and subsequent revisions. General scholarly consensus yields the following dates for the basic time periods:

Middle Bronze Age IIA	ca. 2000–1800/1750
Middle Bronze Age IIB/C	ca. 1800/1750–1550
Late Bronze Age I	ca. 1550–1400
Late Bronze Age II	ca. 1400–1200
Iron Age I	ca. 1200–1000
Iron Age IIA	ca. 1000–925
Iron Age IIB	ca. 925–700
Iron Age IIC	ca. 700–586

For the most part, pottery met basic domestic needs, serving as storage jars, flasks, plates, bowls, and cups. Typical of every household was a set of "common ware." During the period associated with Israel's settlement in the highlands of Canaan's Central Hill County (Iron Age I), these items lacked elaborate decoration. Their styles were standardized to coincide with function (later reflections of this are found in Lam. 4:2; Zech. 14:20). Presumably, the recipe used to mix the clay, including any agents necessary to strengthen it to endure heavy usage, varied according to the type of vessel, although individual potters or villages may have developed specific recipes that they employed for all of their pottery. The collection of pottery in each household included those used for cooking, the storage of grain or other foodstuffs, large jars for olive oil or wine, and lamps. Ceramic containers were supplemented by leather sacks and some carved stone items. While pottery styles did change over time, the common ware tended to remain much the same as long as specific ethnic groups or tribes lived on the site.

Ceramic Typology

Archaeologists catalog the variations in ceramic shape, style, decoration, and firing techniques to create a general typology for each period of the history of the Levant. Among the criteria used for classification are the following:

- style and number of handles
- shape and thickness of rim
- shape and thickness of base
- color and composition of slip used for decoration
- style of incising used for decoration
- distinctive use of geometric, animal, plant, or human patterns of decoration
- craftsmanship and technology
- purpose or function

"Fine ware," fashioned with thinner walls on a fast wheel, becomes more common, especially after the establishment of the Israelite monarchy and the increase in foreign influences (Iron Age II). Like any change in historical period, the creation of new designs or the adoption of foreign designs provide evidence of a shift in society. For instance, these more intricately produced ceramics serve as evidence of greater affluence among people of high status or wealth. Many of these items were carefully shaped of the finest clay available, incised with geometric or zoomorphic designs, covered with specially created colors or "slips" (Prov. 26:23), and set aside for special use by priests (Lev. 14:5; Num. 4:9) or members of the elite classes (2 Sam. 17:28). Particularly fine pieces might survive as heirlooms, as legal storage vessels (Jer. 32:14), or sacred objects for generations. However, the villages and towns of ancient Israel were subject to periodic attack by raiders or invading armies. This resulted in the destruction of homes and possessions and the massacre or deportation of the people. When a site was rebuilt, it might well include new inhabitants who brought with them new pottery types and styles. It is the obvious shifts in pottery typology that archaeologists use to help determine the chronology of both individual sites and the surrounding regions. Thus similar styles and shapes at several sites in a defined area are considered indicative of a common ceramic industry and ethnic identity.

Because potters generally took advantage of local resources, it is fairly easy to determine a pot's origin based on spectrographic or petrographic analysis of the clay. By these means, firing temperatures and conditions as well as the mineral content of the clay are determined, and microscopic organisms or shells are identified. Even if the pot has been shaped and decorated in a foreign style, its clay provides a fingerprint to demonstrate whether it is a local copy or a genuine example of foreign trade. Of course, pottery found its way to new areas in a variety of ways in antiquity: migrants moving into new regions, armies passing through or camping for a time in conquered territories, merchants carrying their goods to foreign markets. Each of these examples provides the occasion for anomalies to appear in the ceramic record. Archaeologists have wondered and argued over the appearance of pottery types in places where they would not be expected. Ultimately, the data allows only basic suppositions to be made about the ceramic record based on the percentage of particular types found. Where unusual items appear, they also provide an opportunity for speculation that may in some cases be coordinated with other artifactual findings and indicate the complexities of reconstructing ancient history and ancient cultures.

Architecture: Domestic and Monumental

Despite the preponderance of attention given to events in the biblical narrative that center around palace and temple, many examples of village life are also included in the narratives, especially in Judges and Ruth. These accounts provide at least brief descriptions of housing and the general layout of the village. They also include the description of agricultural facilities (threshing floor, wine vat, olive press, terraced hillsides, and cisterns) that formed a part of everyday life and became so much a part of life that they could be used as plot details or metaphors by the biblical storytellers and prophets (Judg. 6:1–6, 11; Ruth 3; Isa. 5:1–7). What archaeology has added to this picture is a clear indication that the majority of the people continued to live in small towns and villages even after the establishment of the monarchy. Archaeologists have given greater attention to settlement patterns, and regional surveys have recently dominated scholarly discussions about the social character of Israel's history and the chronology of the monarchic period.

Architecture in all of its forms can also be examined, in much the same way as ceramics, creating a topology of styles, technology, and materials of construction during a series of consecutive time periods. Determination of function leads into conversations about utilization of space, architecture as a form of propaganda, architecture as an expression of ideology, national and individual status, gender roles, evidence of wealth, and cultic activities. Each of these discussions—based on material remains, social theory, and biblical narrative—demonstrates that greater clarity can be achieved when all of the data is brought into play.

Domestic Architecture

During the time associated with the history of ancient Israel (thirteenth to fifth centuries BCE), the most common private dwelling was the pillared, two-story, four-room house. This functionally oriented structure appears throughout the highlands of Canaan and Transjordan in agriculturally based, unwalled villages and small towns. It was well adapted to the environmental conditions of the area, utilizing native materials and a minimum of timber, mostly in the ceilings and roofs. Because the transport of tons of stones and the assembling of four-room houses represented a large investment in time, labor, and materials, these sturdy dwellings speak to the energy of their inhabitants and the desire to provide adequate, permanent shelter for their families as they took possession of the land.

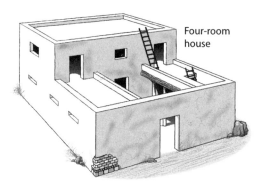

Four-room house

The four-room house allowed extended families to live together and was easily accommodated to the needs of a growing nuclear family (Clark 2003). It consisted of a broad room extending across the back of the structure that opened into three long rooms divided by rows of pillars supporting the ceiling and upper story. There were no windows, and ventilation came from the central chamber or the entranceway. The two outer rooms were often used to house animals or for storage, while the central chamber served as the principle domestic area for the family. Single-storied houses may have had an open, unroofed central chamber to accommodate the smoke from the cooking hearth, but that is still unclear. For two-storied structures, the upper rooms were reached by interior ladders and functioned as sleeping and work areas, with one section unroofed for cooking. The design allowed for some privacy and the designation of specific space for animals separate from the human quarters and the cooking area. Excavations have revealed that the lower walls, built with only shallow or no foundation, were as much as two meters thick. They consisted of rough limestone walls, with the more durable basalt, if available, used for thresholds and doorjambs. The exterior was plastered with lime to prevent erosion. Production of lime was another time-consuming process that added to the expense of the house in terms of labor and diversion from other essential agricultural tasks. The houses were between ten and twelve meters long and approximately eight to ten meters wide. Supported by the thick walls and rows of stone pillars inside the house, the upper story was constructed of mud bricks with lime mortar. Since it was flat, the roof served as additional living space (2 Kings 4:10) and an open-air work area (for drying flax in Josh. 2:6).

In the village setting, archaeologists have found that these houses were often arranged in a series standing next to each other that provided opportunities for social discourse and some protection against raiders. A central area, referred to as a *reḥōb*, functioned as a gathering place for residents and visitors (Deut. 13:16; Judg. 19:15–20). In walled cities, the four-room houses were built against the wall and served along with casemate or hollow sections of the city wall as housing or storage space, accommodating the needs of the populace and facilitating commercial activities (e.g., Rahab's house in Josh. 2:15). Generally, housing was clustered together in the walled towns with very narrow lanes for foot traffic. Any open area would have centered on public buildings (2 Sam. 21:12; 2 Chron. 29:4; Ezra 10:9), but the competition for living space would have kept these squares to a minimum. Most business was therefore conducted near the city gate

(Gen. 19:1) or in small shops built into the homes of their proprietors.

Houses in the Biblical Narrative

Perhaps because houses were simply part of the backdrop of everyday life, there are no explicit descriptions of the steps taken in building a personal dwelling in the biblical narrative. Houses simply existed, and the narratives or legal pronouncements about them mention only certain aspects of a house in the context of telling the story. The insights we can gain on the construction of ancient houses from archaeological excavations create a fuller picture when combined with what little appears in the biblical text. This further highlights our inability to obtain a "Polaroid picture" of ancient Israel's housing situation by simply reading the Bible. Material culture is best studied from material remains.

Deuteronomy 11:20   Covenantal obligation requires every Israelite "house" (i.e., household) to place a scroll on the doorpost of its dwelling.

Deuteronomy 15:16–17   The doorpost is the setting for the ritual of transforming a freed debt slave into a perpetual servant of a household.

Deuteronomy 22:8   Home builders are cautioned to construct a parapet on the roof to prevent anyone from falling and thus incurring the liability attached to bloodguilt (compare the liability law found in the Code of Hammurapi 233, which holds a building contractor responsible for faulty work that resulted in an unsafe wall; Matthews and Benjamin 2006: 113).

Deuteronomy 22:13–21   A woman who has been proven to be unfaithful to her husband is stoned on her father's doorstep.

Deuteronomy 28:30   The litany of curses imposed on violators of the covenant includes the warning that "you shall build a house, but not live in it."

Work Space

One of the things that the work of archaeologists and anthropologists has made clear is that every culture must be examined in the context of all of the varied spaces it occupies. Obviously, the ancient Israelites and their neighbors did not spend all of their time in their homes. The majority of their hours were spent working the fields, herding sheep and goats, processing grain and animal products, and making repairs on their facilities and equipment. Time was also set aside for religious festivals (Lev. 23:2–4; Amos 8:5), marriage ceremonies (Gen. 29:21–22), economic activities, and funerals—each involving different locations and social settings.

Taking this into account, archaeologists have broadened their excavations and surveys to include an analysis of work facilities: silos constructed to store surplus grain, wine and oil presses, cisterns carved into the soft limestone to store water during the dry months of a Mediterranean climate (little or no rain between April and September), and the terraced hillsides that allowed farmers to create arable land to cultivate vines, trees, and grain. Each of these items provides evidence of how the farmers worked to shape their environment and to cope with the limitations placed on them by its ecology and climate.

However, like pottery styles that were used for many generations, the dating of work facilities or the determination of the date at which they were invented or adopted as a worthy innovation is difficult. For instance, there is evidence that terraced hillsides and plastered cisterns existed in the Late Bronze Age in Canaan. The significant increase in their use in the Iron Age I villages of the Central Highlands therefore may simply reflect (1) a continuation of already existing technologies or (2) a realization that they were necessary to meet the needs of the growing number of villages and their populations. Since rural communities tend to be both culturally and ideologically conservative, it could therefore be surmised that even if these villages were built by new peoples (i.e., Israelites) unrelated ethnically to the Canaanites, the decision to adopt this technology and construct terraces was based on a pragmatic conclusion that they would help them survive and grow. The decision to construct terraces on the hillsides also represents a collective decision on the part of the villagers to work together since the vast amount of labor involved in building the terrace walls, transporting topsoil to fill the terrace, and plowing and planting vines or fruit

Work Space in the Biblical Narrative

The most common work spaces in ancient Israel were those associated with agriculture. In some cases archaeologists have been able to discover traces of these installations (pottery embedded in terrace walls, wine or oil presses cut into native limestone) by noting modern use of traditional space in locations that still accommodate the agriculture processes of threshing, winnowing, sieving, and distribution.

Threshing floor A threshing facility was centrally located between adjoining fields or even between villages, functioning as public space. All of the Israelite farmers would have transported stalks of grain to a flat and open space where the prevailing west winds would help in separating the wheat from the chaffs (Job 5:26; Hos. 13:3). After processing, the grain was distributed to the owners, the Levites (Num. 18:27), and the poor. Continuous reliance on the threshing floor as the place of processing and distribution made it the logical place in the village setting to transact business related to the harvest (Ruth 3) and a logical worship area for giving thanks (2 Sam. 24:18–22; Hos. 9:1).

Winepress Archaeological surveys have identified hundreds of small olive and winepresses or vats in the northern and central regions of Canaan. In September (Deut. 16:13), small villages processed their grapes in local winepresses or vats that were cut into the local limestone (Isa. 16:10; 63:3). The treading took place in

▶

trees is the work of many hands, not just one family. Their cooperative efforts built a sense of identity, ownership, and organization that historians and political theorists point to as the foundation for the later establishment of the nation out of these isolated villages.

Monumental Architecture

Because archaeologists work to recover the physical remains of ancient peoples, they occasionally are able to obtain additional information about aspects of monumental architecture from the biblical narrative. Many of the palaces and temples, wall systems, magnificent city gates, and ancillary buildings that housed the members of the priesthood, the royal bureaucracy, and troops were destroyed in antiquity and

Olive press (Courtesy of Jim Yancey)

an upper vat, and the juice was channeled down into a second vat for fermentation and then transferred to jars. Since olives ripened later than grapes, these same facilities could be used to crush olives and extract their juice (Job 24:11). Larger, more elaborate facilities were discovered at urban sites like the Philistine city Tel Miqne–Ekron, which manufactured mass quantities of these products.

Fields Each village was surrounded by fields of wheat and barley. The biblical narrative contains many references to plowing (Deut. 22:10), sowing (Job 4:8; Isa. 28:24), and reaping (Lev. 19:9). Archaeologists may only surmise where these fields lay, but they can investigate the terraced fields constructed in antiquity and maintained for centuries on the hillsides (2 Chron. 26:10; Isa. 5:1–7). The terraces can be assigned a date based on the examination of pottery remains contained in their lower levels, which are comprised of sediments containing a large number of sherds.

their stones robbed out to use in later construction. Often the archaeologist is lucky to find the foundations of these buildings and city structures and must work by extrapolation based on their width and style of construction. This in turn allows for speculation on their height, decoration, and interior design.

The biblical narrative provides a more detailed account of the construction of monumental public buildings, at least to the extent of the materials used and a basic architectural scheme (1 Kings 7:2–7). Scholars who study the development of political systems and the origins of states note that one of the items at the top of a new king's "to-do list" was the construction of monumental buildings that represented both the identity of the nation and reflected his power to command the resources of his subjects and allies (2 Sam.

5:9–12). It is not surprising then that the accounts of the kings of Israel and Judah found in the books of Samuel and Kings demonstrate how building functioned as a form of political propaganda (1 Kings 5–7; 12:25–31; 16:24). While archaeologists have uncovered evidence of some of these massive structures built of quarried and shaped stone, their discoveries do not always coincide with the biblical account, and the dating of these testaments to political and clerical power have created some controversies among scholars.

Chief among the disputes is the tenth-century debate that concerns itself with whether David and Solomon, neither of whom is attested in written records outside the Bible, actually produced massive walled fortifications, palaces, and temples during their reigns. Only the recently discovered Tel Dan Stele, which mentions the "House of David," provides clear evidence of the dynasty founded by David. Furthermore, the lack of archaeological evidence of the temple of Solomon, the royal palace, and other governmental structures has raised additional questions about whether tenth-century Jerusalem was a national capital or simply another hilltop fortress ruled by a chief rather than a monarch. It seems unlikely that a full, indisputable picture of that period will be drawn, since the practice of construction in Jerusalem from earliest times has been to excavate down to bedrock and build of stone rather than mud brick. This means that the archaeological record of ancient Jerusalem, stretching back to the Chalcolithic period (4200–3300 BCE), has been partially destroyed by later builders who removed earlier occupation layers and robbed out stone for their own purposes (Cahill 2003). Added to these difficulties are the present-day restrictions placed on excavating near Jerusalem's Temple Mount district, given the conflicting claims placed upon it by Muslim, Jewish, and Christian groups.

Monumental Structures in the Biblical Narrative

Jerusalem's stepped rampart   Excavations over the past century in the "City of David" down the slope from the Temple Mount have revealed a massive stepped rampart with at least fifty-eight courses in one area approximately seventeen meters high. Dated from pottery recovered in the fill between courses and in probes down to its foundation, the structure was apparently constructed in the transition period between Late Bronze Age II and Iron Age I (ca. twelfth century BCE). It most likely served as a terrace that provided the underpinning for the fortification system and may have in its upper courses provided housing and offices for the city's "administrative-religious complex" (Cahill 2003: 53). The existence of such a structure suggests the importance the city held and adds to the narrative of its use as a capital by David and Solomon. Subsequent construction of

houses on the rampart in Iron Age II indicates that it remained an important feature of the city for centuries.

Six-chambered gates   According to 1 Kings 9:15 Solomon's construction projects included fortifying the important border cities of Hazor, Megiddo, and Gezer. Excavations at each of these sites have revealed massive six-chambered city gates (as in the photo above; courtesy of Chris Miller) that are dated approximately 925 BCE, based on ceramics (red-slipped ware), the campaign records of Pharaoh Sheshonq (Shishak in 1 Kings 11:40), and a destruction layer. While there is no direct historical link between Solomon and these structures, they serve as evidence of the construction of monumental forms of architecture in the tenth century by Israelite monarchs.

Tombs and Burial Customs

Another underreported item in the biblical narrative is the description of tombs and burial customs. To be sure, we have reports on Abraham's purchase of the Cave of Machpelah to serve as a family tomb for his clan (Gen. 23) and the repeated inclusion of a line in the regnal formulas that a king "slept with his ancestors" (1 Kings 14:20) or was "buried with his ancestors in the city of David" (14:31). It seems unlikely, however, that every family could afford to purchase a cave or carve out tombs "on the height . . . in the rock" (Isa. 22:16). The brief reference to the "burial place of the common people" in Jeremiah 26:23 suggests that there was a pauper's field near Jerusalem where criminals or the poor were quickly interred. However, the biblical account indicates that the disgraced (Josh. 8:23–26) or the vanquished (8:29) were given superficial burial under a heap of stones and that the accursed were left unburied as food for scavengers (2 Kings 9:35–37).

Actual details about funerary practices, other than funeral processions and professional mourners (2 Sam. 3:31–34), are very rare (see burning spices in Jer. 34:5). Although the practice is not mentioned in the Old Testament, the application of spices to anoint the corpse and to alleviate the smell (Luke 23:56–24:1) may have been common. A variation on

Reading Tomb and Text

Given the very elaborate grave goods placed in Egyptian tombs and the variety of items included in Middle and Late Bronze Age tombs in Canaan, it is odd that no Old Testament narrative includes any description of the array of objects placed with a corpse in a tomb. There is a general lack of interest in the afterlife, referred to as Sheol ("the Pit") in the text (Job 17:13–16), and necromancy is outlawed (e.g., the witch of Endor and the "raising" of Samuel's spirit in 1 Sam. 28:3–19). Despite this gap in Israel's cultural record, archaeologists have found grave goods to be a means of further dialogue with these ancient people and their understanding of death.

When cooking or storage pots, pilgrim flasks, weapons, jewelry, and foreign items like Egyptian pottery or scarabs appear in a tomb, this raises several questions. Did the deceased and his or her family believe that these objects were necessary to sustain the dead in the afterlife? Were they simply emblematic of the life or gender of the deceased? Because they had belonged to the deceased, had they become unclean (Num. 19:14–16) just as the body of the dead was considered unclean (Lev. 21:1–4)? Did their sacral character diminish over time since tombs were reused many times and other remains were swept aside?

this is the practice of burning incense to honor the ancestors and lament their deaths (Jer. 34:5). Since Saul and his sons are the only persons said to have been cremated (1 Sam. 31:11–13), it is apparent that bodies were placed in their tomb intact, although archaeological evidence demonstrates that tombs were reused over generations and that the remains of earlier burials were swept aside or placed in charnel collections in a side chamber. There is also no mention of what possessions were carried to the tomb with the dead. Given the large variety of grave goods found in excavated tombs (pottery, weapons, jewelry), this is an interesting oversight, although that property did belong to the dead and thus was of no concern to the living. It may be that Job's reference to guarding the tombs of the wicked is related to an attempt to prevent the tombs from being robbed (Job 21:32).

Generally, the place of burial is mentioned (a city or a significant object like the oak near Bethel for Rebekah's maid), and sometimes a tomb was marked with a pillar (Gen. 35:19–20) and became a landmark (Rachel's tomb near Bethlehem; 1 Sam. 10:2). Nonroyal burials are also described as family tombs named for the "father" of the household (Judg. 8:32; 16:31; 2 Sam. 2:32). Preparation of the body, aside from the mummification of Jacob (Gen. 50:2–3) and Joseph (50:26) in Egypt, is seldom mentioned in the Old Testament (compare Luke 23:50–56), although elaborate rituals are outlined for those who have become unclean through contact with the dead (Num. 19:11–22).

With only these brief or passing references, it is not surprising that archaeologists have been able to supply additional information to what we know about ancient burial practices. In agreement with the biblical account, excavators have located many burials in caves and in rock-cut tombs in hillsides. Many of these tombs are clustered together in a cemetery or necropolis with evidence that they have been used over many generations. DNA testing, problematic in remains three thousand to four thousand years old, has not been done on a large enough scale to determine if all are of a single family line. It seems likely that abandoned tombs or the tombs of extinct families may well have been appropriated by others (2 Kings 13:20–21).

Of course, the number of tombs that have been discovered and examined do not reflect the actual size of the population in antiquity. Some tombs have been destroyed by earthquakes, erosion, or robbers. Methods or styles of burial also change over time, and the cost associated with a family tomb may have been beyond the means of many. The lack of a large number of Iron Age I tombs has raised some questions about whether an egalitarian ideal among the Israelite villagers had led them to bury their dead in simple, shallow pits that resulted in the disintegration of the body and the obliteration of the burial site. Others choose not to make conclusions based on a lack of evidence and prefer to continue to collect data and take into account the likelihood that tombs previously dated to Late Bronze Age levels may well have continued to be used by Iron Age I inhabitants.

Inscriptions and Extrabiblical Records

The Bible is not the only written artifact that has survived since the time of ancient Israel. Archaeologists have discovered and linguists have deciphered many extrabiblical documents from Egypt, Mesopotamia, and Syria-Palestine, including royal inscriptions, letters, personal records, epic literature, and economic texts. Some are fragmentary or partially destroyed and have to be pieced together like broken pots. They represent all levels of society, from kings to common soldiers and low-level officials. Each, however, provides a glimpse into the world of ancient Israel and facilitates the dialogue between the modern reader and the scribes, authors, and storytellers who produced them. Like other artifactual evidence, however, they must be treated with care since they can tell only a fraction of the story that led to their creation.

It would be wonderful to be able to ask the writers some basic questions about these compositions: What was the sequence of events that led up to their being written? Who was the original or intended audience? What was edited out, enhanced, or shaped to create the desired effect for the author or the patron who commissioned the inscription or segment of a royal annal? What was in the mind of the royal archivist who collected those items found in the massive library of the Assyrian capital of Nineveh and had them recopied? The questions are endless, and that is as it should be since it is our curiosity about the ancient world that also sparks our interest in a closer study of the ancient Israelites within their social and historical context.

Many extrabiblical texts contribute to our better understanding of epic narratives and historical events and the standard language found in monumental inscriptions, letters, and narratives in the ancient Near East. Although some have no direct parallel to stories in the Bible, they can speak to issues raised about major events in the history of Israel (a topic that will be examined in more detail in chapter 5). While they should not be seen as proof of the historicity of events like the exodus or the conquest of Canaan, they are, like other artifactual evidence, another piece of data to add to our study of these ancient peoples. What they do best is to provide information on the relative importance of the kings of Judah and Israel in relation to the superpower states in Egypt and Mesopotamia and world events that affected the smaller kingdoms of Syria-Palestine.

For instance, the Merneptah Stele is part of a long-standing tradition in Egypt in which the campaign victories of the pharaoh are recorded. Like much Egyptian literature, it follows a standardized pattern. What is helpful to biblical scholars, however, is its inclusion of the ethnic term *Israel*, providing a date (ca. 1208 BCE) for the existence of these people in Canaan. It does not answer the question of whether the exodus from Egypt took place or when the conquest of Canaan might have taken place, but it does add a very interesting piece of chronological data.

A somewhat more concrete example is found in the Assyrian records of King Shalmaneser III (858–824 BCE), whose hegemony extended over all of Syria-Palestine and who was able to extract pledges of loyalty from most of the petty rulers of that region, including King Jehu of Israel (Matthews and Benjamin 2006: 180–81). In Shalmaneser's famous Black Obelisk inscription, Jehu's payment of tribute to the Assyrians is chronicled, and he is depicted bowing down at the feet of the Assyrian monarch, something never mentioned in the biblical account of Jehu's reign. Of course, the Assyrians were not above the use of propaganda to inflate their importance or the degree of control they actually held over other nations. However, given the relative difference in size, wealth, and military power between Israel and Assyria, this portrayal of Jehu's obeisance seems fairly realistic.

Assyrian wall relief: Black Obelisk of Jehu's obeisance

Later inscriptions from ancient Israelite cities, like the Arad and Lachish Letters, provide evidence of a literate society as well as information on the day-to-day activities of a regional center in a time of military crisis. Ration lists indicate diet as well as the degree of comfort these embattled soldiers had. There is even a poignancy to their increasingly desperate situation when they see the watch fires of other military outposts going out and thus can imagine the advance of the enemy toward their position (Lachish Letter 4, in Matthews and Benjamin 2006: 203). Overall, what each of these texts does is give us a better sense of the basic humanity of these people and a feeling that their personal concerns are not that much different from ours or our current national leaders.

Texts from Extrabiblical Sources and Their Biblical Parallels

Extrabiblical Text	Bible Parallels	Description and Comments
Creation Story (*Enūma Eliš*) 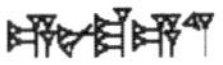	Genesis 1–3	an eighteenth-century BCE description of the emergence of an ordered universe out of watery chaos featuring the triumph of the Babylonian god Marduk
Code of Hammurapi 	Exodus 21–23; Deuteronomy 15–22	commissioned by King Hammurapi of Babylon (eighteenth century BCE), a collection of laws of the *lex talionis* principle that touches on most points of civil law
Merneptah Stele	no direct parallel	a royal inscription of Pharaoh Merneptah (ca. 1208 BCE) listing peoples and places conquered in Canaan, including "Israel"—the first known usage of this name outside the Bible and possibly a key to dating Israel's presence in Canaan in the settlement period
Mesha Stele	Joshua 6:17–21; 1 Kings 16:23–24; 2 Kings 3	a royal inscription of King Mesha of Moab (ninth century BCE) describing how he threw off oppression by the son of King Omri of Israel, destroyed Israelite settlements, and rebuilt cities
Tel Dan Inscription	2 Kings 17:1–18:12	an inscription of King Hazael of Aram (ninth century BCE) describing his defeat of Israel's King Jehoram and the ruler of the "House of David"

Extrabiblical Text	Bible Parallels	Description and Comments
Black Obelisk Relief of Shalmaneser III	no direct parallel	an Assyrian relief (ninth century BCE) depicting and describing how King Jehu of Israel brought tribute to the emperor
Annals of Sargon II	2 Kings 17:5–6	Assyrian royal annals (late eighth century BCE) recording the revolt by Israel and other small states and the subsequent conquest of them and the deportation of their peoples
Annals of Sennacherib	2 Kings 19:14–16	Assyrian royal annals (late eighth century BCE) recording the siege of Jerusalem and Hezekiah's payment of a ransom for the city
Arad Letters	no direct parallel	over two hundred inscriptions on broken pottery recording orders to the military garrison to issue rations, transfer soldiers, and conduct patrols in southern Judah during the sixth century BCE
Lachish Letters	Jeremiah 34:6–7	ostraca inscriptions from the sixth-century BCE garrisons at Lachish and Azekah reporting on conditions during the final days before the Babylonians destroyed these cities and Jerusalem
Cyrus Cylinder	Isaiah 44:24–45:19	a Persian royal inscription (ca. 540 BCE) describing the emperor's capture of Babylon and release of hostage peoples and their gods

In recent years a flurry of new inscriptions have been published, some of which have come under scrutiny because they were purchased on the antiquities market and therefore lack historical provenance, not having been discovered *in situ* by archaeologists. Concerns have also been raised that the purchase of antiquities contributes to the clandestine robbing of tells, destroying any chance of determining the objects' original context. Unauthorized digging must, of course, be discouraged by the scholarly community and by the nations involved. However, the fact remains that it occurs and simply to ignore or to ban publication of any objects or inscriptions of unknown provenance deprives everyone of their value.

To a certain extent the sale of antiquities and the publication of unprovenanced items reflect the continuous and growing interest among the general public for "things biblical," the greed of dealers who wish to obtain high prices for notorious items, the desire of scholars to make a name for themselves, and the desire of museums to boast a richer collection. The notoriety of forgeries does not take away from the importance of the many ancient inscriptions, like the Mesha Stele, which were obtained by purchase and have been authenticated as genuine. Authentication is the key in these cases, and there is the rub. Not every scholar is going to agree on the merits of the epigraphy (writing style and shape) or the surface upon which it is written. Reputations and ideologies are at play, and as a result even greater attention is given to scientific methods of identification. For the student of ancient Israel, these objects, like all other artifacts, are voices from the past. However, they are of no value and cannot be included in the conversation if they are not proven to be authentic.

Conclusion

At the beginning of this chapter the question was asked, How does archaeology contribute to the study of the ancient Israelites? The answer is that the data produced through archaeological excavations and surveys is one of the pieces of the puzzle. Each facet of information adds a dimension to what can be learned through close study and careful attention to details. In order for the work of archaeologists to create as clear a picture as possible, we must listen to and accept the data for what it can tell us and not put words in the mouths of the ancients with our interpretation of what we

---

Opportunities Raised by Archaeology

- Archaeology provides new evidence that assists in reconstructing the world of ancient Israel (i.e., ceramics, architecture, tombs, and inscriptions).
- Material remains provide concrete examples of objects mentioned in the biblical narrative and other ancient Near Eastern texts that advance our understanding of these ancient peoples.
- Because ancient authors, editors, and audiences have an emic (insider) understanding of the setting and details that they include in their literature, archaeology gives insight into some of these difficult passages and fills some of the cultural gaps.
- By including archaeological data, students of ancient Israel can develop a better sense of the characters mentioned in the Bible and other ancient Near Eastern texts as real people who lived, worked, worshiped, and died.
- Archaeology often provides an artifactual and written record of non-elite groups in their life setting in villages and towns.

---

have discovered. Despite archaeology's many contributions to the study of ancient Israel, it has some very real limitations. This double-edged sword can cut through misunderstandings and lead to clear insight, but conversely it can also lead to misinterpretations and a false sense of the truth.

Limitations of Archaeology

- The material remains uncovered by archaeologists are always incomplete.
- Interpretation of artifacts and excavation sites, like interpretation of the biblical text, involves subjective judgments that are vulnerable to revision or being discredited.
- Archaeology cannot prove or disprove the truth of the biblical narrative or its theological statements.
- Archaeological evidence cannot and should not be the only data used to interpret the Bible or the world of ancient Israel.
- Because scientific methods are constantly being improved, archaeological data is subject to reexamination. But even this is not always possible if previous excavators have destroyed data by trying to "get down" to biblical levels or have failed to adequately record and publish the results of their work.

3

Literary Approaches

What insights into ancient Israelite culture can come from a critical study of the Bible and the literature of the ancient Near East?

Now that I have briefly explored aspects of historical geography and archaeological methods, I turn in this chapter to the literature of the ancient Near East, including the story that Israel told about itself in the Hebrew Bible. We are fortunate to have a large body of ancient texts from Israel, Egypt, Mesopotamia, Anatolia (the Hittite kingdom), and Syria. These documents provide evidence of economic activity, diplomatic efforts, administrative techniques, epic literature, poetry, and personal correspondence. They represent the mind as well as the everyday life of these ancient civilizations, and they form an intellectual milieu within which the ancient Israelites conducted their business and personal lives. With that in mind, I intend in this chapter to make use of some of the available corpus of written material from the ancient Near East and to suggest ways in which it can be analyzed and how it can become a central feature of any study of ancient Israel. As I have in other chapters, I will intersperse materials from the other major cultures of the ancient Near East into my discussion of the biblical text. In large part, however, I will depend upon the biblical narrative for many of my examples simply because it is better known and because it contains more specific data on ancient Israel.

Processes and Methods

To understand ancient Near Eastern writers, readers today need to understand the world that they represent and how it is different from our world. For example, concerns over ritual purity and kinship were much more pronounced in ancient Israelite society than they are in our own. In chapter 4 I will present a variety of approaches that have been developed by scholars to reconstruct the world of the ancient Israelites more effectively using social-scientific methods, and these methods generally include close attention to the literary achievements of ancient Israel. In this chapter, the aim is to provide a basic introduction to the various methods used by scholars to analyze ancient Near Eastern literature, including the Hebrew Bible. In this way the body of literature can more effectively be seen to represent a window into our study of the world of ancient Israel. This will involve a description of the methods employed by literary critics and an analysis of the values and limitations of their approaches. Ultimately, I hope to demonstrate that every scholar and student of ancient Israel makes choices about which methods are most useful to them in their reading of ancient texts.

In Chapter 2 I dealt with archaeology and the methods that scientists and historians employ to analyze the material culture and social underpinnings of ancient Israel. For example, among the ancient cuneiform texts discovered by archaeologists in northern Mesopotamia are eighteenth-century BCE letters between the king of Mari and his local governors that discuss the difficulties of coping with tribal groups within the kingdom. In some ways, these texts can help to illumine the stories of the ancestors in Genesis, who also herded sheep and goats and ran afoul of local government authorities (e.g., Abraham's dispute with Abimelech of Gerar over water rights; Matthews 1986). These same texts (from Mari and Genesis) have been examined by scholars through the lenses of more modern ethnographic studies of tribal cultures in the Middle East and Central Asia. However, there are some real limitations in accomplishing this. Religious and cultural traditions in the region have been altered by the introduction of Islam. These seminomadic, tribal-based societies have also, since the First World War (1914–18), been transformed socially and economically by the introduction of new technologies and by cultural assimilation with sedentary cultures. There is nothing quite so disillusioning to a Western eye than seeing a robed Bedouin driving a Toyota pickup with a camel riding in the back!

Given this situation, modern readers and scholars must reconcile themselves to examining these stories from an "outsider" (etic) perspective. Ultimately, we cannot claim to have a "lived" knowledge of ancient Israel or ancient Mesopotamia. Instead we employ a variety of critical approaches to these ancient texts and to the archaeological data supplied by excavating ancient cities and villages, and we openly recognize our limitations. These methods, in turn, allow us to apply social categories to the events described in the narratives and, hopefully, to make those stories come alive for modern readers. Social science methods themselves will be discussed at more length in chapter 4, but listed below are a few of the social categories that appear quite often in ancient stories.

- **power and status**   Kings and priests exercised power, and deference was given to them in speech, manner, gesture (bowing), and general attitude based on their role as the leaders of the community. This deference is also found in official accounts of the reigns of kings, and given this sociopolitical reality their general reliability as complete or even true accounts must be considered.

- **gender** Since Israelite society was basically patriarchal, there were clear differentiations between the genders in terms of jobs (no women served as priests, and nearly all weavers were women), legal standing (only men exercised legal control over land and property), and sexuality (marriages were arranged, and penalties for adultery were harsher for women than men).

- **kinship** Blood ties imposed both social obligations and privileges. In the early monarchy, kings tended to use their relatives (nepotism) in sensitive positions, and in later periods elaborate genealogies were produced to indicate many generations of membership in a priestly family as the basis for service in the temple.

- **clean or unclean** The laws of ritual purity defined persons, animals, and property as either clean (ritually pure) or unclean. Those identified as unclean (e.g., lepers, menstruating women) were restricted from contact with others in the community or participation in religious rites.

Making Effective Use of the Biblical Story

Even though the events described in the biblical narrative occurred thousands of years ago, we hear fragments of the story repeated every day or paraphrased in movies or television dramas or even in the comic strips. Modern novels and plays often rely, whether they are aware of it or not, on story lines from the Bible. Attitudes expressed in sermons, political speeches, and testimony before the courts and Congress are based on or make use of biblical concepts, laws, and situations, which in some cases have their origins in earlier legal or literary texts from Egypt or Mesopotamia (e.g., Code of Hammurapi or Epic of Gilgamesh). Although modern characters in these various productions may not dress like those in the world of ancient Israel, the scenes depicting human ambition and striving, love affairs, and the questioning of the fairness of the world all have their origins in ancient Near Eastern literature. As the author of Ecclesiastes said, "There is nothing new under the sun" (Eccles. 1:9)—at least when it comes to literature, politics, and human dynamics.

With this in mind, it has been my task in this volume to provide a basic guide to resources available to help students of history more effectively understand the world of the ancient Israelites, and a careful study the Old Testament/Hebrew Bible can contribute to this process. Frankly, I would say that one of the easiest ways to draw a reader into the world of the ancient Israelites is by starting with what is most familiar, the Bible itself. Our Bible is filled with all sorts of stories, some edifying and some horrific (e.g., the terrible story of rape and dismemberment in Judg. 19). Many of us have our favorites, but one task of a serious student of the Bible is to become familiar with many of the rest. This does not mean to start at the beginning and read through the text from end to end. While that may serve as a form of spiritual or scholarly exercise, it is not the most effective way to develop a real understanding of what is actually "going on" here. Reading the units as divided by the subtitles in most English-language Bibles will provide a guide and allow one to skip over sections that one may not wish to read the first time through.

Even such a superficial reading, however, clearly demonstrates that studying the Bible is not an easy task. It takes work to identify or even to understand the types of literature encountered along the way. One must be willing to set aside any presuppositions one may have about what is supposed to be in the Bible. It will be difficult to take a strictly chronological approach because the narrative is broken up in places by genealogies, legal materials, and the description of religious rituals and vestments. While one can move from the primordial narratives of Genesis into the stories of Israel's origins and the development of the nation, it will require careful skimming to avoid getting lost in some of the extraneous sections.

To be frank, the editors of the Old Testament/Hebrew Bible were not particularly interested in placing the stories in chronological order. Their agenda included larger matters, such as making the case for their God as the one true deity in a world that tended to think of gods plural rather than a single god. The prophetic literature includes some references to historical events, but again the aim tends to be to remind the people of their obligation as participants in a

---

Basic Tools for Reading the Bible

Study Bible   A study Bible is designed to indicate parallel passages to the reader with an embedded concordance or footnotes on each page that help to explain difficult phrases. With this tool one can quickly move back and forth in the text to see evidence of intertextual connections. It will also contain theological notes for those interested in the development of religious traditions.

One-volume Bible dictionary   With short articles on nearly every name, place, or important concept in the Bible, this tool helps take some of the mystery out of many unfamiliar items and helps tie things together.

Bible atlas   While many Bibles have maps, it is also helpful to have an inexpensive color atlas that graphically demonstrates climate, topography, major cities, trade routes, and the various countries described in the Bible.

Bible concordance   A very useful tool for those looking for a particular passage or doing word studies in English is a Bible concordance. Choose a printed volume or an electronic version to fit your own needs and the translation you use most often.

Translation of ancient Near Eastern texts   Since the Israelites were only one of several cultures in the Near East, it is helpful to have a collection of creation stories, laws, royal annals, and wisdom literature. One such collection is Matthews and Benjamin 2006.

covenant agreement with God (see the discussion in chapter 5 on reading ancient documents as historical). I suggest therefore that one start by reading through the narratives that are already familiar but with a closer eye to detail and with a pen in hand to jot down questions as they arise. A study Bible may suggest parallel passages that will expand interest in the way traditions are echoed or reused in various parts of the Bible. And a good translation of ancient Near Eastern texts that have parallels with biblical narrative and law allows one to see the bigger literary picture.

Ultimately, one's reading of these texts should demonstrate how the various stories function as indicators of ancient cultural values and institutions. In that way, it will be easier to understand how these same stories have been used and continue to be used to shape our own values and in some cases public opinion on sensitive issues.

The Role of the Storyteller

Since the primary source of information that we have about ancient Israel is the Bible, it is a good thing to take note of the process employed by the ancient storytellers who contributed their talents to its composition and editing. These creative agents made conscious decisions as they described the real or created social world their characters inhabit. The simple truth is that how a story is told is often just as crucial as what is said in the story (Coleman 1999: 126). As a result, each story, its words and its structure, serves as an artifact of ancient Israel in the same way that a ceramic pot, a grinding stone, or the foundations of an ancient house attest to the existence of that now extinct society. However, unlike physical remains uncovered in archaeological excavations, the stories have a longer history and may be either a true reflection of the culture as it existed in the time of the storyteller or a perceived understanding of an earlier era by a later editor.

97

While the story purports to describe the time in which the story is set, it may in fact be an artificial setting generated by the mind of the storyteller and simply designed to entertain or be a teaching tool for his audience.

Of course, the difficulty that modern readers have in dealing with the creative process of storytelling is that we lack the "insider" (emic) information that was the cultural heritage of the ancient audience. Emic is a term that anthropologists use to indicate the way members of a culture understand and explain their own society (Harris 1979; Pike 1967). Of course, the ancients did not need to be told every detail of a particular geographic setting, nor would their clothing, gestures, or social relationships need explanation. Social categories or conditions such as power, gender, and kinship, as well as culturally defined states such as clean or unclean, were a part of their everyday lives and could be spoken of obliquely or in a sort of social shorthand by the storyteller without fear of misunderstanding or confusion.

Furthermore, since Hebrew is a language that is very sound-oriented, ancient audiences could derive even more pleasure from well-placed puns (playing on words that sound alike; Williamson 1995), alliterations (in which similar sounding words are used consecutively for artful or sound-effect purposes; Boadt 1983), or onomatopoeia (words whose sound suggests the meaning; Weinstock 1983). The sometimes explosive, staccato rhythms created by employing these language devices added to the aesthetic value of a story or song. In fact, because these stories were all originally part of the oral tradition of the various tribal groups of ancient Israel, much of the fun in telling a story must have resulted from precise or exaggerated inflection, emphasis, and wordplay. Unfortunately, most modern readers do not read Hebrew or Greek and as a result must depend upon the abilities of translators to convey these verbal niceties.

The literature of other ancient Near Eastern peoples is also a source of literary, grammatical, and cultural parallels.

For instance, the similarities between the flood narratives in the eleventh tablet of the Epic of Gilgamesh and the account of Noah (Gen. 6–9) suggest that literary borrowing was not uncommon (Matthews and Benjamin 2006: 27–30). It also is an interesting exercise to compare individual legal statements in the Code of Hammurapi (ca. 1760 BCE) with those found in the Covenant Code (Exod. 21–23) or the Deuteronomic Code (Deut. 12–26) (Matthews and Benjamin 2006: 105–14). However, despite these commonalities with the secular and sacred literature of Egypt, Mesopotamia, and the Syrian sea-port city of Ugarit, ancient Israel also developed some unique cultural concepts that have no parallel elsewhere.

Controversies over Biblical Interpretation

Taking an analytical approach to the Bible has raised controversies among scholars and within various faith communities (House 1992). It is therefore important to understand that critical interpretation does not dismiss the Bible but rather gives a better sense of the real value that the Bible holds for a reconstruction of the world of ancient Israel. Still, without a careful study of the Bible, most of what we can learn about its content is likely to be too superficial. Since the Bible is the basis for faith in Jewish and Christian denominations, there is no reason why its nuances and its historical and literary character should not be examined with a close eye to detail. To obtain full value from the text, critical questions about its sources and the narratives it contains must be raised, or much of its original meaning will be lost or misunderstood (Henige 2005). The writers of the biblical text were not addressing their attention to the people of twenty-first-century America. They were people just like us, with very real, everyday concerns about family, business, the weather, and taxes. Some of what they wrote about themselves and their religious beliefs, especially in the prophetic materials, can be translated into later periods because they hold universal truths. But a great deal in the Bible has no relevance to a modern, industrially based society. The enduring value for this material is found in its contribution to the reconstruction of various aspects of ancient Israelite society.

There has been almost continuous debate during the last two centuries over whether the Bible provides a reliable history of ancient Israel (Thompson 2005; Dever 2004). This increasingly became the case after the discovery and decipherment of the inscriptions of ancient Egypt, Mesopotamia, and Syria-Palestine in the nineteenth century. Scholarly debates raged over the way in which these documents can be or should be used to parallel the stories recorded in the Bible about ancient Israel (Larsen 1995). Coupled with this has been the development of scientific excavation techniques. As noted in chapter 2, these methods now include the incorporation of a multitude of sciences, including biology, chemistry, spectrum analysis, geology, and botany, in the examination of the data coming out of the ground. This broader and more systematic approach has aided archaeology to progress from a stage in the early twentieth century when it was employed primarily to prove the truth of the biblical narrative. Most archaeologists and biblical scholars today realize that it is not possible to prove the Bible through excavation of ancient cities or settlements. They have come to understand instead that this wealth of information is a legitimate means of opening up a better sense of what life was like in the ancient Near East.

The ongoing discussions over epigraphic and archaeological evidence have also coincided with the development of modern biblical criticism and the examination of the text from a literary critical rather than a theological standpoint. Literary criticism attempted to identify and label the genres found in the biblical text and to determine, as much as possible, both the reasons behind the use of particular literary forms and devices as well as the rhetorical artistry of the authors. While some of this simply represents the exercising of scholarly curiosity, much of it was intended to reconstruct the authorial intent and the audience reaction to these poems, songs, stories, and chronicles.

One more recent result of these longstanding scholarly discussions is the division among scholars during the past two decades over what has been termed the maximalist and minimalist approaches to the study of the Bible (compare Davies 2000; Halpern 1999; and Reid 1998). In many ways, this debate is simply an extension of previous arguments and represents the ongoing desire of the scholarly community to understand and assign a historical context to the Bible. Those who consider themselves more attuned to the conservative or maximalist position see no need to restrict their interpretation of the text by applying an overly strict "verification principle" when addressing the historicity of the biblical narrative (Provan, Long, and Longman 2003: 54–56; Millard 1994: 53). This means that for some, it is enough to see the biblical text as a revelation of God's purpose in the world, whether it is addressed to ancient Israel or to modern society. For minimalists, the Bible has become an instrument of political and social repression, justifying colonial landgrabs in the nineteenth century and the repression of native peoples or people of color throughout the world or an icon employed by the church to advance its own agenda and increase its power to persuade its members. Such extreme positions sometimes use the Bible for their own purposes and mask its original meaning behind a facade of piety or demagoguery. Misrepresentation or self-serving agendas need to be recognized for what they are, for they have no legitimate place in biblical studies.

It is not my purpose in this volume to take sides with either the maximalists or the minimalists. However, I do not recommend that the Bible be placed on a pedestal or under glass as if it were a sacred relic that cannot be assailed. I also do not want to discount its potential usefulness as a historical source and as the foundational document of three

Maximalist/Minimalist Controversy

Maximalist approach This position takes the stories in the biblical text from Genesis through 2 Kings at face value, considering them to represent historical truth in every detail. Archaeological and ancient epigraphic evidence is used to bolster this argument in creating a full history of Israel. This means that the interpretation of relevant archaeological and epigraphic data is sometimes shaped to prove the reliability of the biblical story.

Minimalist approach This position attempts to serve as a corrective to what its proponents consider the misuse of the Bible. Seeing no extrabiblical evidence for the existence of any of the characters in the premonarchic and early monarchy periods, they discount the historical reliability of the biblical text. What little that can be written about ancient Israel is culled from Mesopotamian and Egyptian sources with no regard for the biblical account. It is their position that the Bible was not written to convey historical truth but instead functioned as a justification for a religious system developed by the Jewish community in either the Persian (sixth–fourth centuries BCE) or the Hellenistic period (fourth–second centuries BCE). Thus the Bible is an attempt to prevent the assimilation of the Jewish community into Hellenistic culture. The Bible is not a "history of ancient Israel" but a handbook of how to remain authentically and faithfully Jewish.

major Western religions: Judaism, Christianity, and Islam. It is enough to recognize that this set of documents is a very powerful tool for scholars, clergy, and every reader who wishes to learn more about ancient Israel and about the development of a community of faith. Instead, I intend to explain my own interest in the biblical narrative and to provide a basic guide on both how to and why to study the Bible. In the process, I intend to demonstrate how methods of scholarly study allow the Bible to function as a source for ancient history. This survey of methods will therefore begin with a summary of the major approaches to the study of the Bible.

Major Critical Approaches to the Biblical Text

One of the tasks of the modern scholar is to try to determine the literary tools employed by the storyteller and editor, identifying genre, characterization, setting, and, if possible, the purpose for which the story was told and then included in the canonical collection of Scripture. For instance, some scholars utilize social-scientific theory and methods as well as archaeological data in order to come to a satisfactory conclusion about the social world depicted in a particular story. They determine that characters in a story are positioned to fulfill particular and socially recognizable roles. Additionally, since the storyteller is generally attempting to achieve some measure of acceptable reality, this can be reconciled with known social and legal constraints, thereby providing focus to character development and explanations for the forces that shape or demand appropriate behaviors. Given their familiarity with their own culture, the ancient audience could intuit much of what is going on and could even anticipate future action within the story line. They understood power relationships, the implications of conversation, and the relevance of nonhuman entities or conditions to the story. However, it is clear that the storytellers occasionally injected elements that were designed to surprise, shock, or amuse their ancient audience. Sometimes this occurred within the context of what was perceived as "true to life behavior," but sometimes more fantastic settings or events, such as miracles (Josh. 10:12–13), are included in the story line. The full range of storytelling possibilities found in the biblical narrative is a clear indication that these storytellers possessed true versatility and broad understanding of their social world, utilizing it as the natural backdrop to their tales.

Today scholars use a wide variety of critical methods to examine and analyze the biblical text (McKenzie and Haynes 1999; Knight 2004). Through their efforts they attempt to overcome uninformed or slanted interpretations, which are based on misconceptions or biases. Most importantly, they work against the common trend that harmonizes the biblical stories without regard to their social or historical context or any redundancies or discrepancies in the text.

Most scholars realize that it is important to recognize the existence and possible reason for textual gaps, inconsistencies, or contradictions. They see the value in studying and explaining why these textual problems—or, some might say, textual opportunities—exist. In that sense, they may stand outside doctrinal or theologically based interpretations, but their intent is generally to bring out a better understanding of the original meaning and context of the biblical materials, not to attack or disprove the beliefs of any faith community.

It must also be emphasized that few scholars, except those engaged in textual criticism, employ a single method of biblical analysis. Instead, since many of them complement each other, it is natural that they be used in tandem. Several of these methods will be described below, but they might better be termed a scholar's "toolbox." Different tools will be drawn upon to analyze a particular aspect of the biblical text, and eventually the entire set of tools may be used to create a clearer picture of what the text can tell us. Of course, some tools are used more than others in the reconstruction of the world of the ancient Israelites, and some are less favored now than they have been in the past. Although these methods will be referred to as "criticisms," this term does not imply a negative attitude or intent. It merely indicates that the method or criticism is designed to ensure careful analysis and study of the biblical text.

Textual Criticism

Because most modern readers are used to working from translations, they seldom think about the Bible being originally written in Hebrew, Aramaic, and Greek. Unfortunately, we do not possess any of the autographs (original manuscripts) produced by the biblical writers. We are able to study only later copies of these ancient manuscripts. For instance, the Dead Sea Scrolls (dating to 100 BCE to 70 CE) are the oldest surviving copies of the books of the Old Testament/Hebrew

Bible. Every book except Esther is represented among these scrolls, and in some cases there are multiple copies of some books (e.g., Samuel and Isaiah), indicating the popularity and importance of these particular works. Although the Dead Sea Scrolls have defied the elements and the centuries, they still represent only copies of books that originated centuries earlier. Naturally, all of these ancient manuscripts were copied by hand. This means that no matter how careful the copyist or scribe might have been, there will be some differences between manuscripts.

One additional source of information is a small collection of ancient inscriptions found on jewelry, ostraca (broken pieces of pottery such as the Lachish Letters), bullae (clay seal impressions containing the names of their owners), stone pillars or stelae, and monuments (such as the ninth-century BCE Mesha Stele from Moab) that date much closer to the time of the biblical writers. Many of these documents represent invaluable evidence of the writing system of ancient Israel, information on personal names and events, and glimpses into the personal life of the people. However, they are only bits and pieces, the flotsam of history that have somehow survived or been found by chance. They raise our hopes and whet our appetites for more, as we have seen in chapter 2.

Scholars who carefully examine surviving manuscripts and fragments of text are known as text critics (Tov 2001). Comparisons must be made between scrolls, codices, and fragments in all of the original biblical languages—Hebrew, Greek, and Aramaic—and translations in Syriac, Ethiopic, and Latin. Through these comparisons the best possible reconstructions of the original words of the text are made. In the process text critics must make note of and attempt to provide explanations for the obvious errors that have found their way into the text during the copying process over the centuries. Text critics also do comparative work with other languages from the ancient Near East, such as Akkadian,

Examples of Existing Biblical Texts

Septuagint (abbreviated LXX)   When the Hebrew Bible was translated into Greek in the third century BCE to meet the needs of Jewish communities that no longer spoke Hebrew, variations appeared in the stories, based on the use of various textual traditions and manuscripts by the translators and on the cultural and linguistic differences between Greek and Hebrew. Hundreds of Greek manuscripts exist, although none date earlier than the second century CE, and there are variations in these copies based on copyist errors and the favoring of particular manuscripts. For instance, the Greek Orthodox church favors one manuscript, while the Roman church in the West prefers another when making translations from the Septuagint.

Dead Sea Scrolls (abbreviated DSS)   Comprising approximately nine hundred separate documents, these scrolls date to the period between 100 BCE and 70 CE and are primarily written in Hebrew on parchment. They were discovered in 1947, hidden in a group of caves located above the ruins of the Dead Sea settlement of Qumran. Previously, the Leningrad Codex, a Masoretic version of the Hebrew text dating to 1000 CE, had been the oldest copy of the Hebrew Bible in existence. Comparison of the readings found in the Masoretic Text, the Septuagint, and the Qumran materials has contributed to improved translations and has also indicated that the authoritative, canonical text was not yet set at the time that the Qumran scrolls were produced.

Masoretic Text (abbreviated MT)   Hebrew was no longer used as everyday speech following the Babylonian exile and the Persian period (sixth–fifth centuries BCE). It was retained for ritual use and remained the language of the biblical text, except among the Egyptian community, which used the Septuagint. However, ancient Hebrew never developed punctuation or vowel signs. As a result, during the early Middle Ages, approximately 500 CE, a group of Jewish scholars known as the Masoretes created a scribal system of symbols to indicate word division and vowel sounds so future generations would be able to read and pronounce the text correctly. All of these symbols were added in the margins above and below the text, because the Masoretes refused to alter the original text. Many of these Masoretic manuscripts still exist and provide information on the effectiveness of copying such massive documents over the centuries.

Phoenician, Ugaritic, Hittite, Egyptian, and Canaanite dialects like Moabite and Edomite. In some cases this has made it possible to translate Hebrew words that had previously been considered a misspelling or were just unknown. For instance, many words in the Psalms were part of the technical language or jargon associated with the temple choirs and musicians. Some still remain untranslated, their meaning lost or uncertain.

Literary Criticism

Since the Bible is an artifact of ancient Israelite society, it can be studied as a body of ancient literature and can be divided into various literary genres (e.g., short story, poetry, song, prayer, proverb). Using these familiar literary labels can help a modern reader to better identify with the material (Alter 1981). It also allows the reader or scholar to work with the "received text," that is, the version of the text that we now consider reasonably authoritative based on the work of text critics and translators.

Scholars who concentrate their efforts on the literary and historical aspects of the biblical narrative are known as literary critics. Among their concerns are (1) probable authorship and audience, (2) date of composition and/or editing,

---

Assumptions of Literary Critics

Editing process The biblical text did not suddenly appear in its current form. The text evolved over a long period of many centuries from oral tradition and written records. Throughout its development there was continuous editing, based on the following:

1. popularity of the tradition—how well known a story or set of stories were
2. perceived value to the political, social, and religious identity of the people
3. religious and political agenda of the editors in particular periods of Israelite history
4. aesthetic values and creative abilities of the authors and editors

Subjectivity factor No matter how objective a scholar or reader wishes to be when analyzing the biblical text, some degree of subjectivity will find its way into his or her interpretations. The simple fact is that we cannot totally escape our own cultural background, and we cannot fully place ourselves into the world that produced the Bible.

(3) particular literary genre or form of the text, (4) aspects of writing style and structure, and (5) analysis of vocabulary.

Source Criticism

The Bible is like a mosaic floor pieced together with thousands of different colored tiles. Each color represents a tradition or narrative voice that originated with Israelite storytellers from a particular clan or tribe. Centuries after these stories originated, editors laid the tiles or episodes together into a more complete narrative. In so doing, they created a picture of ancient Israel's understanding of its origins and

---

Examples of Source Criticism

Narrative   The flood story contained in Genesis 6–9 contains at least two separate traditions, each of which complements the other in the edited form of the story, but also provides variations in detail. For example, Genesis 6:19 requires Noah to bring "two of every kind" of living thing into the ark, while Genesis 7:2–3 instructs him to take "seven pairs of all clean animals" and "a pair of the animals that are not clean." It could be said the two versions simply go from generic to specific, but it may also represent a later writer/editor who was concerned with sacrifice and purity issues. Some of the details contained in at least one of these traditions closely parallels the flood story in the much older Epic of Gilgamesh, but it is clear that the Israelite editors have reshaped this story to fit their own understanding of the reasons for the flood.

Law   The legal materials found in Exodus 21–23 (Covenant Code) represent an earlier stage in the cultural history of Israel than those found in Deuteronomy 12–26 (Deuteronomic Code). Furthermore, the Holiness Code found in Leviticus 17–26 is clearly associated with the priestly community of the postexilic period (ca. 500 BCE) and shares only the category of "law" with earlier codes, not their social and historical context. An example is the shift in the village law on debt slavery (Exod. 21:2–3), which probably dates to the tenth century BCE and originally set the term of only six years of service, but adds a stipulation in the later version (Deut. 15:12–15) enjoining the creditor to provide "liberally" out of his bounty so that the slave can make a fresh start. The text also adds the typically Deuteronomic (sixth-century) explanation for this change, citing Israel's slavery in Egypt and God's redemption and care for them.

---

identity. Scholars who study these various voices within the text are known as source critics (Sommer 2006). Source critics attempt to develop a set of criteria for each source so that it can then be identified amid the threads of a story. For example, some traditions may use particular names for God (Elohim, El Elyon, El Shaddai, Yahweh), while others emphasize particular cultural, geographic (northern or southern kingdom), or religious aspects of their society (forms of ritual, sacrifice, purity regulations). Once this analysis is done, it becomes fairly apparent that the text is too complex for it to be attributed to a single author or a single time period. There are simply too many instances in which information does not fit the social or chronological context of Israel's early history. The stories and legal materials that have been woven together represent a variety of viewpoints (geographic, ethnic, social) and different time periods.

Form Criticism

As a result, and rather than trying to explain away inconsistencies or redundancies in these narratives, the reader is better served by learning to appreciate the diversity of the biblical traditions and the skill employed by the editors in blending the disparate materials together. It can therefore be helpful to break the text down into smaller, identifiable units known as pericopes, based on such things as language style (meter, size of stanzas, and rhyme) and specific literary genres. By establishing the defined limits for these units or pericopes, the reader is better able to classify them as particular forms, such as lament (Ps. 22; 137; Lam. 1), parable (2 Sam. 12:1–4), fable (Judg. 9:8–15), song (Exod. 15:1–18; Judg. 5), or hymn of thanksgiving (Ps. 18; 92).

Scholars who employ this method are known as form critics. For them, it is important to make an effort to determine the life setting or social context of the storyteller or community that produced this textual segment (Melugin 2003). The form critic also speculates on the factors that influenced the author or editor to use particular genres or forms. In other words, what occasion in the life of the people at a particular stage in their history required them to compose and sing a hymn of victory (Exod. 15:1–18), formulate a law on building standards (Deut. 22:8), commemorate a major historical event with a song (Judg. 5), create a ritual celebrating the coronation of a king (Ps. 72), or chant a lament describing the destruction of a city (Ps. 44; 137)? Of course, this entails a great deal of speculation and reconstruction and works best when combined with social-scientific methods.

Tradition Criticism

Since these smaller units eventually had to be joined together or embedded into larger narratives to create the fuller biblical story, an editing process must have taken place. Of course, we do not have the notes from the minutes of the meetings held by these editors. All we have is the received text and the ability to examine it with a sharp eye to detail. The analysis of the editing process is similar to the work of archaeologists in the sense that it attempts to determine the points or literary strata where one tradition has been replaced or merged with another later one. As will be noted in chapter 5, the editors are engaging in a retelling of the story, what Paul Ricoeur (1995: 184–85) calls the process of "narrativization." Thus the theological perspective, the cultural biases, and sociopolitical agendas of a later period combine to reshape earlier materials to produce a new "sign" or interpretation.

Scholars who employ this method are referred to as traditio-historical critics (New Testament scholars use the term *redaction criticism*). These individuals look for evidence demonstrating how stories have been spliced together or shaped to create a particular viewpoint of events in the story (Stone 1997). These critics attempt to identify the "footnotes" or

Examples of Tradition Criticism

Modern translators indicate textual glosses or additions that biblical editors or ancient scribes embedded into the biblical text by placing them in parentheses. It is also possible to identify the methods that editors used to link text together and to insert their political or religious agenda as asides into the text. Tradition critics use these glosses as one means of identifying the editing process and the date when that might have occurred.

Genesis 2:24   Following the story of the creation of Eve in Genesis 2:18–23, a social gloss was added: "Therefore a man leaves his father and his mother and clings to his wife, and they become one flesh." While this fits the social context of later periods in Israel's history and provides a legal and cultural explanation of marriage, it has no direct relation to the story in Genesis. It functions here as an editorial aside commenting on a later social development made possible by the creation of Eve.

Genesis 32:32   As part of the narrative describing Jacob's return to Canaan, Jacob is forced to wrestle with a divine being at the Jabbok River (Gen. 32:22–31). A later editor appended a postscript to the story that includes a dietary statute restricting the consumption of "the thigh muscle that is on the hip socket." This postscript is another example of the way in which a later editor or redactor, probably a priest in this case who is concerned with ritual purity, makes use of story elements to make a legal or social judgment about community behavior.

Exodus 3:14–15   Sometimes in a complex narrative an editor finds it necessary to create linkages between segments. In this example, two distinct responses by God to Moses's question are linked by the redactor with the phrase "God also said to Moses." In this way two sources or traditions of the story have been spliced together to provide additional responses to Moses's question about God's name.

Judges 19:10   Since it is possible that the ancient name of Jerusalem may not have been known to its later inhabitants, the redactor inserted that information into this story about a journey in which the people "arrived opposite Jebus (that is, Jerusalem)."

1 Kings 16:25–26   Looking back on the history of Israel, the sixth-century BCE redactor known as the Deuteronomistic Historian colors the chronicle of the history of the kings of Israel and Judah with value judgments like that found here, describing how Omri "did more evil than all who were before him. For he walked in all the way of Jeroboam son of Nebat." A similar statement indicting the people of Israel is found in 2 Kings 17:7 explaining that they had been conquered by the Assyrians because they "had sinned against the Lord their God." In this way, historical events are couched in terms of divine decisions or actions.

"editorial fingerprints" that appear in the text. Some of this is rather mechanical, and readers should be warned that not all redactional features of a text are designed to make a theological point. They may simply be a means of achieving a smoother-flowing narrative or providing a later audience with information so that they will not be confused by archaic terms.

In addition, tradition critics attempt to suggest the possible motivation of the editors or redactors for inserting information or crafting a narrative in a specific manner. For instance, one of the major redactors is identified as the Deuteronomistic Historian (Campbell and O'Brien 2000). This person (or group of persons) is generally considered to have lived in the sixth century BCE at the end of the monarchy period or during the early exilic period. Concerns over the destruction of Jerusalem, the end of the monarchy, and the exile of the people of Judah to Babylonia are the motivation for the manner in which he (they) shaped the "history" of Israel in the books from Joshua through 2 Kings. In particular, the emphasis on the "pollution" of the northern monarchy by the "sins of Jeroboam" (1 Kings 12:25–33) serves as a theological overlay on what may have originally been the archival records of the kings of Israel (Auld 2000: 360–61).

Narrative Criticism

Turning to the story itself, a more familiar method for analyzing the text as a whole is known as narrative criticism. The object here is to employ a close reading of an entire story identifying plot features (type-scenes, dialogue, and repetition) and the elements associated with characterization, rhetorical style, themes, and motifs and then to speculate on the author's "intention" and the text's "original" audience (Gunn 1999). There is less emphasis or interest among narrative critics on the historical features or context of the text. Their primary interest is in its literary features and the likely effect that the story has on it audience and readers. The assumption is that it would have been the goal of the ancient storyteller or narrator to draw the ancient audience into the story by creating a lively plot with interesting characters. The narrative critic's job is then to identify and analyze the setting, conflicts and crises, role of the narrator, and the use of stylistic features. Instead of being concerned with authorship, the narrative critic strives to establish the point of view of the narrator and the likely reaction of the implied audience being influenced by the elements of the story. Despite this emphasis on the literary character of the text, a wealth of social-world information can be drawn from the stories, and this in turn, if not the direct intent of the narrative critic, can contribute to a reconstruction of the history and society of ancient Israel.

Structural Criticism

Of course, many literary units in the biblical text can be identified based on their structure. Genealogies, royal annals, poetry, folk tales, and myths follow particular patterns and contain what structural critics call universal elements. Scholars who employ structuralism as a method of interpretation focus on what most would consider impersonal and universal codes in the text (Jobling 1995). For example, every culture produces stories of a hero's quest. And each of these stories contains certain universally accepted elements that move the narrative along toward its completion (Cohn 1982): (1) a disruption of the status quo that sets the story in motion, (2) the equipping and/or persuasion of the hero that propels him into battle against the forces of evil or disruption, (3) the battle in which the hero defeats evil and restores the status quo, and (4) the hero's return home or to a stable life. When this structuralist method is applied to the story of Elijah's confrontation with Ahab in 1 Kings 17–19 (see sidebar), a familiar pattern emerges from the story elements.

113

Elijah/Yahweh versus Ahab/Baal

Disruption of status quo (1 Kings 16:31–33; 17:1–24)   The story begins with Ahab's willingness to supplant Yahweh worship in Israel with his Phoenician wife's Baal worship. To indicate that a crisis has been precipitated by this act, Elijah is sent by God to combat this evil influence on the nation and to serve as Yahweh's champion in the confrontation that is sure to occur. Elijah is initially equipped to handle the situation with a message forecasting a three-year drought (17:1). This is not only a calamity for the farmers who depend upon consistent rainfall to ensure a bountiful harvest, but it is also a direct challenge to the powers of the storm god Baal. Furthermore, the prophet is sent to Zarephath in Phoenicia, where he restores an impoverished household (headed by a widow) to life by providing a jar of meal that is never empty and by reviving the widow's son from a mortal illness (17:17–24). This is, of course, the opposite of what is happening in Israel, which is faced with famine and death during the drought.

Equipping and/or persuasion of the hero (1 Kings 17:17–18:1)   The revival of the widow's son and her declaration that "now I know that you are a man of God" (17:24) functions as a reinforcement of God's initial call for Elijah to take actions that mirror the coming of the drought and the return of life with the aid of Yahweh (17:3–5, 8). Then, after the three years have passed, God puts Elijah in motion once again to stage a contest with Ahab's 450 prophets of Baal on Mount Carmel.

Battle in which the hero defeats evil and restores status quo (1 Kings 18:8–45)   The public contest before the assembly of the people gathered around the mountain makes it clear which god has real power and/or desire to respond to the prayers of his followers. This victory for Yahweh is marked by a formal acknowledgment by the people that "the Lord indeed is God" (18:39), a massacre of the false prophets (18:40), and the end of the life-killing drought (18:41–45).

The hero's return home (1 Kings 19:4–18; 2 Kings 2:1–12)   Although Elijah is forced to flee from Jezebel's wrath after his victory at Mount Carmel (1 Kings 19:1–3), he is subsequently called to further service while dwelling on Mount Horeb, a place where God's presence is felt (19:4–18), and is finally "taken home" when God plucks him from the earth (2 Kings 2:1–12).

This is only one possible structuring of the events in this story. Other interpretations could picture Ahab as a failed hero, unable to carry out the quest of restoring Yahweh worship, while yet another places the people into the collective position as the hero, who in the end reject Baal (massacring the prophets of that false god) and thus restore harmony.

One thing that structuralism does is to take the reader/audience out of the picture since it is based on the art of composition and editing. Its scientific, mechanistic approach is concerned with how the story is put together and how it follows the conventions of composition; it is unconcerned with how the story may be received. This approach breaks down, however, when it is applied to more complex narratives that cannot be subdivided so easily and that are not dependent on set patterns or rigid structures.

Rhetorical Criticism

Another facet of narrative criticism is the examination of the rhetorical character of a particular story or literary unit. Rhetorical devices or techniques determine the structural features of a text and identify the literary or poetical devices that function as rhetorical tools, such as repetition, parallelism, analogy, and inclusio. This analysis also includes speculation on the original author's intent in using these devices, but some rhetorical critics choose to take a purely descriptive route, steering clear of any discussion of authorship or purpose beyond the artistic. What is clear is that rhetorical situations are described in the text. For instance, during the crisis period following King Josiah's death in 609 BCE, the prophet Jeremiah goes to the gate of the temple in Jerusalem on a festival day and proclaims his message of warning, calling on the people within earshot to "amend your ways" so that God will be able to continue to dwell among them (Jer. 7:1–4). While there is an actual audience in the story, it can be speculated that Jeremiah was not speaking just to those who happened to be there that day. His use of familiar prophetic themes, the repetition and rhythm of his statements, and the immediate effect that they had on "the priests and the prophets and all the people" (26:7–9) all suggest that this moment in time would be repeated and reinterpreted by many other audiences when they faced similar

115

situations. The issue raised, therefore, is the implicit ideology of Yahweh-only worship advocated by the prophet and the call to obey their covenantal obligation that is embedded in Jeremiah's sermon. The rhetorical critic would want to explore not only the mechanics of his speech but also how these impacted and interacted with the socially preconditioned experiences of the audience, both in the late seventh century BCE as well as in later periods (J. Willis 1985).

Reader-Response Criticism

Reader-response criticism attempts to explore how both ancient and modern "interpretive communities" interact with the text. For these scholars the meaning of a biblical story or its interpretation by the audience/reader (ancient or modern) is variable, depending upon the background and perspective of that group or individual reader. For some this means that the text diminishes in importance as the role of the reader increases. As a result, it is only what the reader or interpretive community says about a text that matters. Such a radical reading of the narrative, however, may too easily set aside its original social and historical context and promote the idea that it is unnecessary for the reader to be concerned with any meaning other than that created by the mind of the reader. For those who profitably use reader-response criticism, there is a balance that accepts the value attached to the intentions of both the implied author, who is working within a particular historical framework, and the implied reader, who may be concerned with the ancient literary and historical context or have a modern perspective on the text.

Canonical Criticism

A somewhat related method of interpretation is known as canonical criticism, which is also concerned with the influence that the body of biblical writings has on a community,

---

Reader-Response Approach
(based on Briggs 2002)

Using the Genesis creation story as an example, reader-response critics suggest three categories of investigation or inquiry that take into account parallel creation stories from the ancient Near East. They are aided by "sensitization" to the way in which narrative functions in general, to the function of science in prompting us to ask questions about reality, and to the breadth of ancient literature as an influence on the "implied author's" creative process:

1. **Some issues raised by modern readers have no direct connection to the story created by the ancient author(s)** This includes current scientific questions about the big bang theory, the evolutionary process, and the various eras in which the dinosaurs reigned over the earth. Both Genesis and other ancient creation stories such as the Babylonian "Creation Story" (Matthews and Benjamin 2006: 11–20) and the Egyptian "Hymn to Ptah" (Matthews and Benjamin 2006: 3–6) are silent on these matters because they either involve data unknown to the ancients (Israelite, Egyptian, or Mesopotamian) or are irrelevant to their story of the origin of the universe since they may not involve divine action.

2. **Some issues are of interest to both the ancient and the modern reader** For example, Genesis 2:24 provides an explanation for the social practice of a newly married couple establishing their own distinct household, separate from their parents and in which they "become one flesh" both physically and legally. The dynamics of marriage and its social and legal character are still of great interest in current society.

3. **Some issues of great interest to the people of the ancient Near East have no direct relevance to modern readers** Thus the Genesis creation story makes very clear that God created all of the facets of the universe (sun, moon, stars) and that these objects are not deities themselves. There is no sun god, river god, or sea god—only Yahweh. This polemic against the polytheistic religions of Egypt and Mesopotamia represents a fight that is no longer relevant in modern Western culture.

---

specifically the community of believers within a tradition of faith (Barton 2003; Chilton 1997). Among the most important questions raised by the canonical critic is this: How and why and when did this text gain canonical status as a sacred text? While some attention is given in this method

117

to the process that led to the creation of the received text, it is more concerned with the forces within the faith community that helped shape the development of the canon of Scriptures. It also takes into account how different phases in the history of the nation have impacted both the telling of and the final formulation of the text. These scholars also draw on other critical methods such as redaction, source, and historical criticism to bolster their interpretation of these events. This allows for the identification of different traditions within the narrative (such as the two creation accounts in Gen. 1:1–2:4a and 2:4b–25), but a conscious decision is made to listen to the entire story rather than fixating on its disparate pieces. Furthermore, there is no insistence that the biblical text is a "sourcebook" for the history of ancient Israel. Rather it is considered to be a reflection of the sense of identity put forth by the community of faith at various times throughout history as it draws on the biblical materials to express its beliefs and values.

Canonical critics also emphasize that the biblical materials have acquired an additional dimension during the process of transmission and the formation of the Scriptures. This separate dimension is based in large part on the use that faith communities make of these narratives. The very recognition of a set of Scriptures by a faith community potentially invests those materials with a larger audience, but one that reads the texts in a particular way, either in Bible study or in liturgy. As such they are less concerned with the original intent or purpose of the authors and more with the way in which the texts speak to people today.

There also can be a greater sense of rigidity of interpretation in the canonical approach since the transmission process has established a particular order for the texts. Not every canon is precisely the same: the Christian canon and the Hebrew canon do not follow the same book order. The Jewish Bible places the Writings (Psalms, Proverbs, Job, etc.) in its final section and thus concludes the total message of the

Bible with Cyrus's release of the exiles from Babylon and a call for the Lord's people to "go up" and rebuild the temple in Jerusalem (2 Chron. 36:22–23; compare Cyrus's own rendition of these events in Matthews and Benjamin 2006: 207–9). This is a very different conclusion than that in the Christian Old Testament canon, which concludes with the reference to the return of the prophet Elijah as a harbinger of the coming Messiah (Mal. 4:5–6). The point is that once a canon has been set, both readers and scholars begin to analyze it according to its set order and to investigate why certain books or narratives may have been placed in a particular position.

Social-Scientific Criticism

Since chapter 4 provides a fuller discussion of social-scientific criticism, I will simply note here that this method employs a multidisciplinary approach, taking advantage of the theoretical models created by psychology, sociology, and anthropology. Its primary aim is to explore the social dimensions evident in the biblical narrative (Halligan 2003; Chalcraft 1997). This method sometimes provides a means of recreating ancient social situations through the analysis of rhetorical, economic, political, and social forces. Its interpretations also take into account human reactions to particular social and environmental conditions and physical and psychological stresses. For example, the political and psychological dislocation caused by Absalom's revolt against his father David and the preparations taken by the king for his subsequent flight from Jerusalem (2 Sam. 15–16) can be explored in terms of its effect on the participants as well as on the audience who hears or reads this story.

Ideological Criticism

The final category of interpretation that I want to introduce here is that of ideological criticism. While some define this method as an artificial, even a harsh treatment of the text, it is in fact the application of some social-science methods as well as modern political theories to the social world portrayed or even hidden in the biblical narrative (Penchansky 1992). Ideological critics recognize that the biblical material was composed within a social setting that emphasized the role of the male character, of the elite members of society, and of certain ethnic or national groups (Yee 2003). Because of this "repressive" forces are at work, both in the ancient composition process and in the later reading and interpretation of the narrative. Ideological critics assume that background characters or groups have been intentionally ignored and

Feminist Criticism

The task of the feminist critic is to identify and trace the forces in society that suppress a woman's ability to be a full participant. The male-oriented ideology, androcentrism, expressed in the Bible places an emphasis on the activities, ideas, and roles of men. Feminists judge this to be sexist when it serves as the ideological basis for the exclusion of women, based on their gender alone, from public participation in legal, economic, and religious matters. Some feminist interpretations that discuss or emphasize these aspects of ancient Israelite society as revealed in the text have examined the following:

1. women as victims of rape (Tamar in 2 Sam. 13:1–22), violence (Levite's concubine in Judg. 19:22–30), and judicial shaming (accused wife in Num. 5:11–31)
2. women who make accommodations to androcentric ideologies (childless Hannah in 1 Sam. 1:3–8 prays for a son in order to obtain greater esteem within her husband's household and a higher status among his fellow wives who have produced children)
3. women who emerge from fragmentary traditions as major leaders (Moses's sister Miriam has apparently been submerged in the narrative by her brother's tradition, and her actual role in ancient Israel can be pieced together only from fragments like Exod. 15:20; Num. 12:1–15; 20:1; and Mic. 6:4)
4. women whose voices replace those of a silent or foolish male (Abigail in 1 Sam. 25:14–38 takes the place of her husband Nabal, who has foolishly scorned David's requests for supplies and has endangered his household; see Matthews 1994)

should be brought to light and given the attention that they deserve. For example, feminist criticism often takes an ideological approach. Feminist critics attempt to demonstrate that women in the ancient world were a powerful force in their society and that their influence helped to shape its culture as well as the biblical narrative. Examples of this appear in the ancestral narratives, in Judges, and in the historical narrative of Samuel–Kings, where women often have strong roles that emerge once the traditional chauvinistic biases of some scholars or theologians are set aside.

It is in fact the biased reading that limits the power or role of characters in the biblical narrative that ideological critics attempt to overcome. Their aim is to provide a reading that liberates the text from cultural presuppositions about gender, race, class, or nationality. Sometimes the questions that are asked by these critics call for a reexamination of a narrative based on what is missing from the story. Why are certain characters nameless or silent? Why do some characters take the lead in the narrative while others are passive or even missing from major scenes? What are the economic forces that drive the storytelling or the interpretation of the story? Most of all, ideological critics take the position that there are no nonideological readings and that no readings or interpretations of the Bible lack a political agenda or political consequence.

An Informed Reading

I do not want to give the impression after surveying these various methods of interpretation that the biblical narrative is too complex for the casual reader or new student to understand. These many paths of interpretation are simply avenues to explore aspects of the world and the intellectual traditions of ancient Israel. Some may be useful and others may not. What I am advocating is that the serious student of the Bible should become an informed reader. Acquire the tools, both intellectual (a basic knowledge of historical geography, archaeology, social theory, and historiography) and mechanical (atlas, study Bible, etc.), that will make reading a richer experience and that will demonstrate more clearly the value of biblical studies for the reconstruction of the world of ancient Israel. In this chapter, I have tried to tie together portions of what has been discussed in more detail in several other chapters in this volume and to show the importance of a close reading of the text using various literary methods. This may seem somewhat sterile and analytical at times because we tend to categorize or label things. However, it should also be enjoyable. Wonderful stories, excellent poetry, and heartfelt emotions are expressed in these texts, and they are worth reading and rereading.

4

Social Sciences

How can the social sciences help us reconstruct the world of the ancient Israelites?

As I noted in chapter 2, archaeologists create relative chronologies for each site by documenting the artifacts, architectural features, geologic data, and organic remains. In the process they place every find into an interpretative matrix out of which conclusions will be drawn about the inhabitants of the site and their history. Dating of physical objects, such as an ancient cooking pot, is based on the excavation stratum or layer within which that object is found. Of course, a cooking pot—like every other artifact—also has a cultural setting that is a factor in reading the history of the people that produced and used it. For instance, a thorough examination of the pot and the stratum in which it was discovered may suggest (1) that these ancient people had a local pottery-making industry, (2) that they had developed methods to cook their food, (3) that they may have delegated certain domestic tasks to particular persons, and (4) that they may have chosen to share their food with neighbors or guests or

Sociological and Anthropological Terminology

Although some of the terms listed below deal specifically with biological ties or survival techniques, each is a factor in the regulation of social behavior.

Honor and shame   These concepts are two sides to the same cultural coin, and they function within a Mediterranean culture like that of ancient Israel as incentives for "correct" behavior as defined by their community and as disincentives to "incorrect" behavior. Striving to be honorable or to acquire honor is status building for both the individual and the household. Shame attaches to every member of a household if any member engages in speech or action that threatens their honorable state or endangers the existence of the household.

Kinship   Every person has a network of associations based on blood relations, commercial ties, political alliances, or membership within a particular community. All of these can be defined in kinship terms, although the strongest are blood ties, and identifiable households (*bêt ʾābôt*) are the standard social unit. Each social tie is also associated with recognized social obligations that govern behavior. There may be some confusion in reading ancient literature because social labels such as *father* and *son* may refer to blood kinship, political status, or economic alliances.

Reciprocity   Social behavior and economic strategies are often governed by the principle of reciprocity. This concept—which relates to such cultural activities as patron-client arrangements, gift-giving, and hospitality—centers on the desire to obtain a balanced return for effort expended. A patron does not accept the loyalty and labor of a client out of charity but rather to gain an economic or political advantage. The most common practice is to give a gift and expect to receive a gift of similar value in return. Honor is to be gained by offering hospitality to a stranger and by following the social protocol assigned to the roles of host and guest.

may have decided how large a group may eat together at one time. The latter two suggestions take us into the sociological realm and beyond the simple utilitarian role of the cooking pot. They touch on issues of gender roles, hospitality customs, and social obligation within an extended kinship or clan group.

Of course, ancient Israelite culture no longer exists, and its members cannot be observed or interviewed to obtain firsthand information on their reaction to everyday events in

▶
Ritual Everyone engages in a personal routine and in communal rituals of passage. These consist of speech, gestures, or actions that are repeated daily or on a regular schedule and collectively serve as cultural identity markers. The simple pattern of getting up at dawn, performing necessary bodily functions, eating a meal, and working until sunset establishes a sense of place within a community. Collective actions associated with religious practice, because they also follow a set pattern at a prescribed time, serve the same function.

Socially shared cognition This concept occurs when a group of people collectively and automatically recognizes and understands the meaning and identity of a visual cultural icon (e.g., Santa Claus). If a widow appears in a story, the assumption will be that she is dressed in "widow's garments." However, that character can be transformed, despite her actual status as a widow, by changing into another costume and therefore creating a social mask and a new public identity (e.g., Tamar in Gen. 38:14–15). A similar transformation takes place in a Ugaritic epic (ca. fifteenth century BCE) when Paghat disguises herself as a prostitute but is wearing male clothing under her female garments as part of her plan to avenge her slain brother Aqhat (Matthews and Benjamin 2006: 78–79).

Liminal People in every culture undergo social and physical transitions. For instance, a child moves into adolescence but is not considered to be an adult. A woman loses her husband or goes through menopause and her status changes as well as the way other people view her. When people are in this in-between state, no longer fitting into their former social category, they are liminal (neither this nor that). Places, like the ruined cities mentioned in the ancient "Lament for Ur" (Matthews and Benjamin 2006: 249–50) or the book of Lamentations, can also be liminal. A threshold is neither in nor out of a house; it is that transition point between them.

their lives. As a result, reconstruction of their emic (insider) viewpoint becomes a matter of interpretation and is subject to the degree of objectivity that the researcher can apply to the biblical text and to available archaeological data. For as Louis Jonker notes, "interpretation does not take place in a vacuum" (2000: 1).

In order for the outsider to even begin to reconstruct an emic perspective based on the artifactual remains of an ancient culture, certain recognizable social terms, concepts, and values must become a part of the process. The etic ("outsider" or observer) interpreter then can make claims about cultural acts as described in the narrative or extrapolated from examination of a physical artifact. Although this is never an entirely objective process, the data can be refocused and its meaning clarified on a sort of universal cultural scale. What I hope to demonstrate is that even though we cannot fully understand the ancient Israelite emic perspective on beliefs and actions, there is still a possibility of deriving insights into what the insiders can tell us about their world. Again, I must note that although I will draw on materials from several ancient Near Eastern cultures, much of the discussion in this chapter will center on the biblical narrative because of its basic familiarity to readers and its importance to a social reconstruction of the world of ancient Israel.

Emic and Etic Perspective

Since the Bible is also a cultural artifact, this same process of sociological speculation, based on close examination of the text, can be applied to it. The distinctive layers of cultural meaning identified in the biblical narrative and other ancient literature can serve as a key to a more effective reconstruction of the world of the ancient Israelite. The social context presented in these texts is revealed as its layers are stripped away in much the same way that an archaeologist strips away the soil in an excavation. Cultural signposts come into view, or social indicators embedded in the narratives suggest when a story may have been composed as well as the worldview and social customs of the time in which the episode is set. This requires that the reader become more culturally conscious. By this I mean that the reader should be more sensitive to references to everyday-life items such as clothing, food, aspects of travel, marriage customs, as well as those places described in the text as particularly significant to the lives of the people.

Given that Israelite culture as reflected in the biblical tradition and the cultural context of the ancient Near East in which that tradition developed are not always the same, attention also needs to be given to the perspective of the author/editor. This is because the manner in which that person or persons composed, recited, recorded, or shaped a story was based on their particular cultural background at the time that they contributed to the development of the story. In fact, as long as the material was still in oral form, perhaps recited or performed by professional storytellers, local elders, or members of a household, it would have been shaped to fit the social understanding and experience of their audience. The basic story line would have remained the same, but settings might be altered, the names of heroes or villains changed, and explanations added when archaic elements were no longer understood. This same shaping process took place when these stories were written down and ultimately became set in canonical form. For example, editorial glosses added to the text are designed to explain a city's name change (Judg. 19:10), to provide clarification of a legal pronouncement (Deut. 22:19), or to point out the effect an action has on the people in later periods (Judg. 18:30). Much of this editing was done in order to better serve the needs of the faith community that used these narratives as part of their religious rituals and identity creation and thus has a social function of facilitation of understanding. And, of course, some of the intentional shaping of information took place to fit the political and religious agendas of the editors and their patrons in successive eras (Jonker 2000).

All of this editorial activity adds to the layering of the text, and it all has a cultural foundation that can be explored. Even when cultural information is masked or obscured, no longer reflecting its original social setting because of the intrusive efforts of later editors, interpretative keys still remain to be examined. If nothing else, the repeated shifting of elements in the story, the updating of obscure references with glosses or footnotes, and the shaping of the material over the centuries tells us about the process that led to formation of the canonical text.

However, a sociological reading of an ancient text is not always an easy task. Cultural meaning is sometimes embedded in a story in a very offhanded manner, and we may not immediately catch it. This is in fact a reflection of the emic ("insider") perspective of the storyteller at work. In our modern Western society, few of us have an intimate knowledge or understanding of life in a small (one hundred to two hundred people) agricultural community that depends for its survival on the rains coming in their proper season (Mediterranean climate brings the rains in the fall and winter) and the harvest producing enough to sustain them throughout the coming year. Furthermore, since our society tends to glorify the individual, we find it difficult to think in terms of the group unless we are a member of the military, a sports team, or a large extended family. This makes us less sensitive to the cultural nuances contained in these ancient narratives, and it requires us to set aside our modern preconceptions about what life was like in ancient times.

In chapter 3 I explained that modern literary critics have provided maps, guidebooks, and charts that attempt to identify these separate layers and the editing process that produced them. This is an important task, but it is one that cannot be complete until the cultural layering is identified and taken into account. These layers are reflections of how the narrative has been shaped by a series of authors and editors who embedded aspects of their cultural context into the story—even though this may have occurred centuries after the original storyteller lived. Furthermore, the social perspective of the original audience and their reactions to the narrative would have been based on their culturally defined norms, values, and language. Later audiences, including modern readers, react to the same narrative based upon their cultural setting and viewpoint, which is likely to be very different from that of the ancient audience (Eilberg-Schwartz 1990: 97–100).

Caution must also be exercised so that in this process of interpretation and reconstruction we do not fall into the trap of simply becoming "passive documenters of indigenous claims" (McCutcheon 1999: 17–18). The ancient writers tell us what they wish to tell us, and they seldom explain everyday acts or behaviors. These are so much a part of their own world that they would consider explanations to be redundant to their audience. Furthermore, this mundane data may not serve the purposes of their account. By unpacking the text and trying to discover the emic meaning behind what the writer considered common knowledge, the modern researcher also discovers some of the reasons why the story was told at all and why it was told in that particular way.

It must also be recognized that social customs change over time, and it is only through the identification of these changes that the social scientist can trace the cultural evolution evident in the text. Admittedly, emic interpretations are no more valid than etic interpretations of a tradition. Therefore, I am not going to try to reconstruct either the etic or the emic understanding of the tradition. Instead, I wish to help people in one time and place—today—accurately understand people of another time and place—the world of ancient Israel.

Methods of Interpretation

Since the 1970s social-scientific critics have placed their emphasis on the application of sociological and anthropological methods, in conjunction with the field of ethnoarchaeology (David and Kramer 2001). The delineation of social models allows researchers of ancient Near Eastern

Models of Sociological Interpretation

Structural-functionalist approach   With its foundations in the work of Émile Durkheim (1954) and A. R. Radcliffe-Brown (1952), this approach takes the position that all aspects of a culture interrelate and therefore cannot be understood except as components of the overall structure of a society (McNutt 1999: 20–21). Each facet of a culture contributes to the advancement and stability of the society as a whole and thus works toward equilibrium through consensus building. When conflict occurs, the forces calling for change can either be absorbed into an acceptable and recognizable social structure or denounced and outlawed as a danger to society. How a society copes with these social stresses says a great deal about its stability, flexibility, and resilience or resistance to change. The chief value in examining a culture from a functionalist viewpoint is in its emphasis on analyzing a culture as an interrelated whole, categorizing its structure, and establishing the relationships between various facets of the society (e.g., kinship patterns, economic system) and actual behaviors of the inhabitants (Mayes 1989: 105–13). However, there is also a tendency to limit the perspective and the study of a culture to a particular period. This does not allow sufficient latitude to deal with a culture with a long history and multiple social transitions.

Conflict theory   Originally formulated by Georg Hegel and Karl Marx and adapted by Max Weber, conflict theory examines forces within a society that either contribute to or promote conflict between the classes or structures of a society (Collins 1994). At work are ideological differences on how to control the means of power and the modes of production. It is therefore necessary to first identify competing groups within the society. The task is then to analyze their

▶

literature to identify common and apparently unique cultural elements and behaviors. While some studies choose to look at isolated cultural phenomena, it is more common to find comparative studies (e.g., Talmon 1978; Fiensy 1987). Some investigations are designed to examine cultural concepts over long or short periods of time, such as Mary Douglas's study of the conceptions behind the heightened concerns with ritual impurity in the Levitical code (Douglas 1966: 41–57). Others concentrate on particular regions or make comparisons between cultures in widely dispersed areas. The social structures that make up society—from the family unit methods for either protecting their own interests or supplanting the assets of other groups. The assumption is that the potential for social change and social conflict is endemic within every society. The only way that this potential for flux or open conflict can be avoided is through methods of constraint. An ordered society is one, therefore, that has achieved control over the forces of conflict by coming to know and understand their potential for violence, channeling their energies into less revolutionary pursuits (Malina 1982: 233–35). The assumption that this model applies to all human societies, regardless of time period, does not take into account all possible variations.

Cultural materialist theories   Scholars may classify societies based on their modes of subsistence (hunting and gathering, pastoral nomadism, agriculture) and on the technologies they develop to take better advantage of the natural resources of the area they inhabit (Lenski, Nolan, and Lenski 1995: 78–91). Evolutionary processes are posited that allow a shift from classless, egalitarian societies sharing resources into rigidly stratified societies dominated by those who control the modes of production. According to this position, ancient Israel underwent a cultural transformation from a village-based society to an urban-based society, dominated by a centralized authority (Gottwald 1979b). There is also a sense of environmental determinism inherent to this position since it bases cultural development on the opportunities and limitations of the topography of the culture zone (Harris 1979: 56–58). The danger with this type of classification, however, is found in a too-rigid approach that does not always allow for multiple economic endeavors (Hopkins 1987). Few farmers live exclusively off their crops. They balance the risk by keeping a few sheep and goats or by engaging in small cottage industries.

to the ruling elites—can be studied in the light of historical data and from a macroorganizational perspective (Lenski, Nolan, and Lenski 1995).

It is apparent that no one social-science model can be touted as the most reliable or most useful for the reconstruction of the ancient world. Instead, while scholars may favor a particular method or theory, most choose to take a more eclectic approach, applying a variety of social theories to what is revealed by the ancient textual material and the exposed archaeological data. Most also recognize that building a social model of an ancient culture based on information drawn from the study of modern cultures has its dangers. Presuppositions or the desire to make the data fit the chosen model simply discredit the process (Herion 1986; Carter 1996: 23–28). However, a careful application of these models can be useful in tying data together. By taking a more objective stance on the relative value of these models, the researcher and the reader can engage in continuous self-evaluation and a restructuring of the interpretative approach as needed.

With this in mind, I will now ask several questions about the usefulness of applying social models to the biblical text. The object will be to provide some insights into the social context evident in the narrative and to make the reader more conscious of the cultural code of these ancient Israelite writers.

Questions Based on Social Interpretation

What Story Elements Contribute to Social Interpretation or Reconstruction?

The answer to this question requires the dissection of the narrative, drawing out and listing social markers and elements of everyday life, as well as the physical and cultural setting. The story of David's confrontation with Goliath serves as a good example (see sidebar).

How Can Significant Space Be a Catalyst in the Narrative or an Indicator of Social Values and Practices?

Humans conduct their business within defined physical space (Matthews 2003a). They socialize and carry out family tasks in their homes. Farmers go into the fields to plow, sow, and cultivate their crops. Merchants set up booths to sell their wares. Kings sit on their thrones dispensing justice and making policy decisions. In every case, these acts take place on

David and Goliath

1. **Physical setting** The Philistines are encamped "at Socoh, which belongs to Judah" (thus within Israelite tribal holdings, not on Philistine ground), "between Socoh and Azekah, in Ephes-dammim" (1 Sam. 17:1). Saul's forces are encamped "in the valley of Elah" (17:2). Because the Elah Valley opens into the Coastal Plain controlled by the Philistines, this means that the setting for the duel between David and Goliath is on a threshold or liminal spot, which would be an appropriate locale for a battle that will determine who will control the Shephelah and dominate the commerce between the Hill Country and the Coastal Plain (2 Chron. 28:18 provides later confirmation of this).

2. **Cultural signpost** The challenge by the Philistine champion, Goliath, calls on the "servants of Saul" to "choose a man . . . and let him come down to me . . . that we may fight together" (1 Sam. 17:8–10). This type of contest between single champions or heroes to decide a battle is not typical of Israelite warfare (the one variation on this theme is found in 2 Sam. 2:12–17, where the contest involves twelve against twelve), although it does occur in legal disputes between households (Ruth 4 illustrates the process with regard to levirate obligation). However, it occurs several times in Homer's *Iliad* and may be an indicator that the Philistines are descendants of a people related to Greek/Mycenaean culture. Thus it is not so strange to read that Goliath's challenge caused the Israelites to be "dismayed and greatly afraid" (1 Sam. 17:11). This was not only a physical clash, but a cultural clash as well, and a contest between gods.

3. **Physical description** The opponents are complete opposites and a total mismatch:

Goliath	David
six cubits + a span high equals 9.5 feet (1 Sam. 17:4)	"just a boy" (1 Sam. 17:33), youngest son of Jesse, not yet military age
armor includes bronze helmet, coat of mail weighing 5,000 shekels (125 pounds), bronze greaves on his legs (1 Sam. 17:5–6)	Saul's armor (bronze helmet, coat of mail) too heavy for David to wear (1 Sam. 17:39)
weapons include bronze-headed javelin, massive spear with iron head (weighing 15 pounds), shield-bearer (1 Sam. 17:6–7)	Saul's sword too heavy for David, replaced with David's staff, his sling, and five stones picked up from the wadi (1 Sam. 17:40)

▶ From a literary standpoint, this technique is an "underdog motif," which heightens tension in the story and fulfills David's words in 1 Samuel 17:37 that "The Lord, who saved me from the paw of the lion and from the paw of the bear, will save me from the hand of this Philistine." From a social-world perspective, the important elements are related to material culture and ethnicity. Based on his armor and weapons, Goliath and, by extension, the Philistines are a rich people with a high level of technology. David discounts this technological advance, using a cultural slur, "uncircumcised," for the Philistines and expressing dismay that the Israelites and their God were being shamed by the enemy's defiance (17:26). Honor and shame are extremely important concepts in ancient Israel at every level of society. What magnifies this situation is the potential that Israel's God will be shamed, at least according to Goliath, if they do not accept the challenge.

4. **Labeling**   David's taunting of the Philistines as "uncircumcised" and therefore not part of the covenant community (see Gen. 17:10–14; Judg. 14:3) is a direct response and balance to Goliath's scornful baiting of the Israelites, calling on them to show enough courage to send out "a man" to face him in combat. Enemy nations use unflattering terms for each other, an exercise in "insider/outsider" verbal jousting (Judg. 14:3; 15:18; 1 Sam. 14:6). Labeling Goliath and, by extension, all Philistines as "uncircumcised" functions as an ethnic slur and marks him as an outsider, who should be given no occasion to rejoice over the misfortunes or weakness of Israel (compare David's eulogy for Saul in 2 Sam. 1:20). In the prophetic literature the label *uncircumcised* becomes synonymous with ritually unclean (Isa. 52:1) and those cursed by God (Ezek. 28:10).

5. **Political element**   This story goes beyond the challenge to single combat. Saul, who had been chosen king and previously distinguished himself as war chief (1 Sam. 11), is shamed and politically diminished by his willingness to accept David as Israel's champion. Clearly, the point is being made that David dares to do what Saul does not. In addition, a social model of courage and faith in the power of God to protect faithful members of the covenant community is created here (17:31–37). It is counterbalanced in a later portion of the narrative that notes Saul's failure to show such faith (28:3). Even Saul's attempt to "clothe" David fails (17:38–39). This is an interesting turn of events since the recognized authority figure who normally invests his subordinates with power to act for him (compare Joseph and the pharaoh in Gen. 41:40–45) provides inappropriate vestments of power that must be cast

▶ aside, leaving Saul without anything to gain if David is victorious. In essence, each character undergoes a social transformation, a reversal of roles. David stands in the contest with only what he had brought with him, his sling, and Saul stands on the sidelines while someone else fights his battle.

6. **Shaming speech**   A second round of taunting occurs as the two champions meet (compare 2 Sam. 5:6–8). Goliath claims he is shamed, treated like a "dog," because he faces an unarmed boy. He follows this with a curse, a practice intended to highlight violation of covenant agreements and a means of bringing down retribution on the head of the violator (references in Mesopotamian texts use the term *māmītu* for the curse as well as the demon that is engendered by the breaking of an oath; Geller 1995: 49). Goliath swears to leave the boy's body unburied and food for the birds and animals (1 Sam. 17:43–44). This particular curse makes sense only if his culture values proper burial (compare Elijah's curse of Ahab in 1 Kings 21:21–24). David's response perfectly balances Goliath's threats, pointing out how useless the Philistine's weapons are in the face of God's power and predicting Goliath's death and the transformation of the Philistine army into carrion for the animals to feed on (1 Sam. 17:45–47). To add another dimension to this rhetoric, it should be noted that the public display of enemy bodies is commonly reported in the Neo-Assyrian annals (see the Kurkh Monolith of Shalmaneser III in Hallo and Younger 1997–2002: 2.261–64 §113A).

7. **Rhetoric**   From a rhetorical perspective, David's statements are far too eloquent for a mere boy, and it seems unusual that his bold words would be repeated to King Saul (1 Sam. 17:31). This suggests a political agenda at work in the narrative by either the authors or editors of the story. Scholars refer to this story and the extended narrative in 1 Samuel 16–2 Samuel 10 as the "apology of David," a carefully crafted piece focusing on why David and his family had the divine right to seize the throne from Saul.

8. **Reversal**   The actual fight between David and Goliath is very brief and anticlimactic. David simply stuns the slow-moving giant with a stone from his sling and then cuts off the Philistine's head while he lies turtlelike, unable to get to his feet (1 Sam. 17:48–51). Using Goliath's sword to behead him is poetic justice, since the people who lacked the technology of warfare prevail (see 13:19–22 for Israel's lack of metal smithing), turning the enemy's weapon and their reliance on technology against them. It also reinforces the underdog motif so prevalent in Israelite narratives in which the weak prevail against overwhelming odds.

or within recognized spaces. In order to provide some categories for the different types of space that we inhabit, I
will use the term *first space* to identify those concrete items
that can be mapped and that we determine to be geophysi-
cal realities (Berquist 2002: 19). Although not part of the
physical universe, we also conceive of "imagined space," in
other words "ideas about space" or imaginary or idealized
space (i.e., Eden), which can be referred to as *second space*.
Finally, *third space* can be thought of as "lived space" where
communal activity occurs (Flanagan 1999; Gunn 2000:
157–59). Applying these concepts, it becomes possible to
classify how space is associated with events, legal formula-
tions, architectural design, political boundaries, behavior,
and personal ambitions.

Space, once it has become culturally defined, further
defines those who utilize or interact with it (Eliade 1959).
Thus, for example, the entrance to a temple marks the
transition point in space between the sacred and secular
world. Someone who stands in that strategic space and gives
a speech (such as Jeremiah's temple sermons in Jer. 7 and
Jer. 26) obtains an enhanced social definition in distinction
to that same person standing in the middle of an empty
field and making the same speech. The cultural character
of the temple threshold, while neither fully sacred nor fully
secular—and thus a liminal or culturally ambivalent location—transforms the person that stands there along with
his or her words into someone and something of heightened
importance. In the case of Jeremiah, it increased the extent
to which he was perceived to be a threat to the temple
authorities and required them to take drastic action in
order to silence him. His use or usurpation of what they
considered to be their "private space" or "sphere of authority" threatened them and gave him "discursive authority"
(i.e., the effect he had on his audience; see Lincoln 1994:
10). It required the authorities to take action, first with a

trial (Jer. 26:7–19) and later by placing him in the stocks (20:1–2).

Of course, every society and every group (male or female, free or slave, king or peasant) forms its own concepts of space, and thus these concepts will vary from one society to another. As a result, lived space (those places in which human occupations and activities occur) becomes the basis of group identity and social boundaries. It can therefore be said that "by acting in space in a particular way the actor is inserted into a particular relation with [his or her society's] ideology" (Cresswell 1996: 17). For example, in the Middle Assyrian Law Code, if a prostitute or a slave is seen wearing a veil in public, then she is to be charged for this illegal practice at "the palace gate," have her clothing confiscated, suffer a flogging, and have tar poured in her hair (Matthews and Benjamin 2006: 126). She has violated established dress codes, impersonated a free woman, and flaunted her crime in public space.

Physical space is continuously redefined by human presence and individual interpretation of the ideology of place. For instance, the view of a field by a farm worker evokes particular connotations: how it can be planted, contoured, irrigated, made more productive. On the other hand, that same field, when viewed by a real-estate developer is first mentally and then physically transformed into plots of land for houses, schools, parks, and commercial establishments. To demonstrate this social phenomenon in which physical space is redefined, we will analyze two commonly used public places: the city gate and the threshing floor (see sidebars for discussions of each of these).

Perhaps the ultimate expression of authority, blending significant space with other icons of power, is found in the story of the confrontation between two kings, Ahab and Jehoshaphat, and the prophet Micaiah in 1 Kings 22. The narrative is based on a situation (22:3) in which the northern kingdom of Israel has lost a piece of territory (Ramoth-gilead)

City Gate

- A city gate is an intentional opening in the wall that surrounds and protects a settlement.
- The gate functions as one facet of the city's defense system (Josh. 2:5; 2 Sam. 11:23).
- The gate area provides a setting for business and legal transactions and an assembly point for the city elders or a king (Deut. 21:19; 1 Kings 22:10; Prov. 31:23).
- Only free citizens have the right to pass in and out of a gate without question or examination (Gen. 23:10).
- The gate, like the threshold of a private dwelling, is a liminal juncture, separating the safe or familiar world and the dangerous or foreign outside world (Judg. 9:35–40; Prov. 18:10).

Having determined that the city gate has a practical function, allowing entrance into and exit from the city and serving as an open space for business activity, we can now turn to the apparent social functions of this defined space. To do this we will examine some of the ways in which the city gate is embedded into the biblical narrative as a story element:

- Lot sits in the gate at Sodom (Gen. 19:1). By placing him here the biblical writer indicates Lot's social status and thus identifies him as an accepted member of the community, even though he is a resident alien, a *gûr* (19:9). He has been granted the right to conduct business in a space recognized by the community as suitable for business transactions. As every person engaged in business knows, a high-traffic area with clear visibility of one's wares is very desirable. However, there are legal and social limits to this status, as Lot discovers when he attempts to protect his guests.
- Boaz calls on Bethlehem's village elders to gather at the city gate to witness the testimony of Naomi's levir (Ruth 4:1–2). Boaz had come to the gate because

to the neighboring kingdom of Aram (Syria). At this point, Judah is allied to and subservient politically to Israel. Thus Jehoshaphat of Judah acknowledges his vassal status with a pledge of covenant fidelity: "I am as you are; my people are your people, my horses are your horses" (22:4). Before they go to war, however, standard procedure is to "inquire first for the word of the LORD" (22:5) to ensure that the Divine Warrior will aid them (22:13; compare Judg. 18:5).

▶ the elders would have to pass him to get to their fields, and the gate is a space that has come to be recognized and accepted by the people as a place where economic and legal practices can be conducted publicly (Matthews 1987).

- The rebellious son is brought before the elders at the city gate. His parents testify against him and the citizens stone him (Deut. 21:18–21). Legal procedures require a defined space that the community has identified as being communal, thus symbolic of their collective presence and authority to act in the protection of their lives (compare the placement of the heads of Ahab's "sons" at the gate of Samaria in 2 Kings 10:8). Just as the gate area has advantages for business owners, it literally provides the space necessary for a public gathering. However, for it to function as a place of justice, it must become socially acceptable. The convenience of a high-traffic area to gather witnesses and elders may serve as a factor in this identification, but this is coupled with the security function of the gate as a defensive installation and with its association with freedom and citizenship.

- Jeremiah stages an execration ritual at the "entry of the Potsherd Gate" in Jerusalem in order to place a curse on the city (Jer. 19:1–13). Like the episode of the rebellious son mentioned above, Jeremiah casts judgment in a place most intimately associated with the crime committed. The rebellious son had harmed the entire community by his refusal to obey the command to "honor your father and your mother" (Exod. 20:12). Thus, his execution in the space identified by the people as symbolic of their unity, strength, and prosperity was appropriate since his actions jeopardized all of these qualities. Jeremiah's condemnation of the people of Jerusalem is made in a place associated with their idolatrous practices. Thus, their inappropriate use of the space given to the Israelites by Yahweh required a gesture that both signaled an end to divine patience and was recognizable as a form of cursing in the ancient Near East.

Ahab's four hundred court prophets are consulted, and their unanimous response is, "Go up; for the LORD will give it into the hand of the king" (1 Kings 22:6).

Such a positive omen from the mouths of men who are in the employ of the king does not satisfy Jehoshaphat, and he asks that an unaffiliated prophetic voice be consulted. Apparently, Ahab needed Judah's troops to carry out his mission and therefore acquiesced, although he complains that the man "never prophesies anything favorable about me" (22:8). The prophet Micaiah ben Imlah is summoned, and at this point a sociological interpretation of events becomes particularly helpful.

In this instance, the task of the social-scientific critic is almost like peeling away the layers of a cultural artichoke. Each level of authority associated with furniture, clothing, place, and entourage is evident in this verse. And, it all hinges on an understanding by the ancient Israelites of the political value attached to a place (city gate built on a threshing floor) that is associated with the security and work of the people, their economic prosperity, fair dealings under established, customary laws and traditions, and covenantal ties to maintain a just society.

Needless to say, Ahab's intent in setting up this space-based meeting plays upon the various popular understand-

---

Socially Significant Elements in 1 Kings 22:10

What makes a king a king? Heredity, success in war or diplomacy, and general acumen are contributing factors, and all play into society's stereotype (visual and mental) of a king. One model for a king's power and person is found in the Prologue to the Code of Hammurapi, where that monarch adopts titles like "good shepherd," "raging bull," "wise mediator," and "deliverer" (Matthews and Benjamin 2006: 106). However, a king's authority is also derived from a set of physical objects associated with his person: robes of office, throne, scepter, crown. A king must in fact look the part. In addition, the king's person transforms the space he occupies and imbues it with his authority. Likewise, space that already is considered significant simply adds to the power of the king when he performs an official act in that place (Allen 1999: 196). In 1 Kings 22:10, Ahab and Jehoshaphat enhance their authority by using the following physical objects.

- Royal thrones are placed in the gate of Israel's capital city of Samaria on a site that had previously been a threshing floor—a quadrupling of authoritative symbols and places.
- The kings wear their royal robes—clothing that they alone can wear and that is a recognizable symbol of their power.
- The four hundred court prophets are arrayed around the thrones and are publicly prophesying.

ings of this place's symbolic value. His actions may seem quite crass, but, like any good politician, he understands the importance of proper placement and setting. He has taken advantage of the social space that he, as king, is apparently free to manipulate. While the gate area is associated with the movement of the citizens in and out of the city and is therefore an integrated place where persons of various social classes may come into contact, Ahab has been able to draw upon its character as a source of power. It thus becomes an extension of his own personal court, a much more restricted social space (Matthews and Benjamin 1993: 122–24).

In this way, what in physical space was inherently open to free commerce by all free persons and by its nature is socially mixed has become, at least temporarily, in both physical and social space an area controlled by the power emanating from two monarchs, their trappings, and their court temporarily removed to this outdoor location. By utilizing a high-traffic area, such as the city gate, the kings can take advantage of the combination of forces and events to create a designed effect.

The threshing floor and its physical characteristics are also used by the biblical storyteller. In the village culture, which lacked walled cities and therefore did not have a city gate, the threshing floor became more than just a communal place of work for processing grain. It was socially redefined as a place intimately associated with the harvest and thus with the future plans of the community (Borowski 1987: 59–62). Here the past year comes to an end, and a new year joyously begins (see the harvest celebrations in Isa. 9:3 and Ps. 126:5) when harvesting and herding are done, bills are paid, and all debts are reconciled. The heads of households start the cycle once again by establishing contracts to breed and graze their herds, to obtain seed grain, and to use additional laborers to work their crops.

Threshing Floor

- As we know from ancient Egyptian wall paintings (Eighteenth Dynasty, Theban Tomb of Djeserkaresonb; T. James 1984: 124) and its use by modern villagers in the Middle East, the threshing floor is a large, centrally located, flat space that is open to prevailing winds and therefore suitable for teams of oxen to be hitched to a threshing sled and driven over the stalks of grain.
- Farmers in the village culture of ancient Israel brought their harvested stalks of grain to a communal threshing floor (Deut. 16:13).
- Farmers processed the grain on the threshing floor using a threshing sled to separate the stalks or chaff from the grain (2 Sam. 24:22). This was followed by a winnowing and sieving process that eventually resulted in piles of grain arranged around the facility (Ruth 3:7).
- Since the threshing floor is usually a communal installation, it is liminal space, a neutral spot in which negotiations and legal transactions can take place.

The economic understandings associated with this process include the determination of property rights based on the amount of grain brought by the harvesters. However, an additional formula also comes into play designed to provide for the powerless groups in society: widows, orphans, freed slaves, and strangers. For instance, when an Israelite debt slave has completed six years of labor and is freed in the seventh year, the law mandates that he or she should not be sent out "empty-handed" (Deut. 15:12–15; compare Code of Hammurapi 117, in Matthews and Benjamin 2006: 109). Instead, the slave is given a financial stake from the flock, from the threshing floor, and from the winepress. This is simply one of many examples in which the threshing floor and the winepress are coupled as economic indicators of prosperity or the abundance of the land that in turn is to be distributed to its people, to the Levites, and, in this case, to freed debt slaves (Num. 18:27; Deut. 16:13; 2 Kings 6:27).

Still, this does not exhaust the social implications of the threshing floor. In 2 Samuel 24:18–25, David goes to the threshing floor of Araunah following a plague and carries out a business transaction there, purchasing that property as well as the animals for sacrifice to mark the end of the calamity. The transactional dialogue in this text is very similar to that between Abraham and Ephron the Hittite in Genesis 23:10–16. In both cases an emergency (a death and a plague) has necessitated purchase of land, and in both cases the owner is a non-Israelite (a Hittite and a Jebusite) who begins the dialogue by making a magnanimous gesture, offering to freely give what the petitioner asks to purchase.

While this could be identified as normal bargaining strategy, the object is real estate. Land is sacred and seldom sold (especially to someone who is not a member of the family or the defined insider group; see 1 Kings 21:1–3). What makes this transaction remarkable is a transfer of the use of space in perpetuity (third-space qualities). David had previously taken possession of Jebus, Araunah's city, by force (2 Sam. 5:6–10), but in this case he must request a sale. There is also a formal transfer of its physical dimensions (first-space qualities), which would be determined by the placing of boundary stones (Deut. 19:14). For legal purposes, there must be no possibility of future claims being made against the land or the recipient. Finally, the second-space aspects of the transaction encompass the idea of the cave and adjoining land, and its social connotations as a family burial chamber determines its place within society and ultimately forms a bond that is linked to membership in the covenant community.

What Can Sociological Interpretation Tell Us about the Political Character of Ancient Israel as Portrayed in the Biblical Narrative?

Ongoing studies of Israel's origins and its eventual political evolution into a chiefdom under the leadership of Saul and David and then into a monarchy in Solomon's reign have built upon or responded to the work of Norman Gottwald (1979b). Although Gottwald's economic-determinist model has been strenuously critiqued (Sasson 1981; Herion 1986), his careful delineation of the social facets of ancient Israel (from its tribal structure patterns to its modes of subsistence management) have guided many scholars over the last three decades. For instance, Frank Frick points to better management of natural resources, improvements in technology, and the resulting economic surpluses attendant with population growth as a combination of factors leading to the development of a chiefdom and eventual political stability under the leadership of a single family (Frick 1985).

Numerous archaeological surveys and excavations by Israel Finkelstein (1988, 1995), Lawrence E. Stager (1985), and others in Israel and Jordan over the last three decades have helped to support this widening social perspective and have pointed to the necessity for a multifaceted approach to the reconstruction of cultural and political development (Esler and Hagedorn 2006: 26). As noted in chapter 1, archaeological surveys that map entire regions are an excellent source of information on settlement patterns and land use. Adding to this increasing store of data from which to draw conclusions and form interpretations of the world of the Bible is the helpful explanation by David Hopkins of geomorphology, climatic studies, and agricultural economic principles. His study of the evidence recovered in excavations and surveys of the village sites in the Central Hill Country dating to the Iron Age I period has added an important dimension to social-world studies (Hopkins 1985).

Taking what we have learned from surveys and applicable methods, let us now turn to the biblical text. The narrative in 1 Samuel 9–11 contains an etiological story of the transition from the anarchic judges period to the introduction of a chiefdom under the leadership of Saul. Since this account was reworked a number of times by tenth- and ninth-century court scribes and by the sixth-century Deuteronomistic Historian, its reliability as a strictly historical account is doubtful, but it does have real value as a study in the social dynamics of power. Thus the underlying political forces at work can

---

Saul Becomes Chief

Samuel's sons abuse their power and the people call for a king (1 Sam. 8:3–5) Underlying this situation is a lack of coordination among the tribes and their elders that is made worse by military pressure from the Philistines (4:1–11), population growth among the Israelites that demanded the expansion into new territory, and the need to deal diplomatically with other nations (8:19–20). The tribal elders respond to a common threat and relinquish some of their authority in order to obtain greater stability and military protection (T. Willis 2001: 29).

Samuel raises the issue of abuse of power by kings (1 Sam. 8:11–18) In what is clearly an assessment of the monarchy based on the later actions of the kings of Israel and Judah (e.g., 1 Kings 5:13–18) as well as an antimonarchy strand that runs throughout the narrative in Samuel–Kings (e.g., 1 Kings 15:26; 16:30), the political realities of giving up personal freedoms in exchange for security and stability are spelled out.

Samuel, at God's command, anoints Saul "ruler over his people Israel" (1 Sam. 10:1) Authority is invested in a person by the consent of the people and certified by public ritual acts. In this case, there is a further certification based on a socially shaped understanding of the extreme value attached to olive oil. The ritual of anointing with oil, because it is a staple of the economy, is performed at the command of the deity, implying divine-right rule and a reiteration of the covenant promise of fertility for the people and the land.

Saul's military victory over the Ammonites solidifies his position as chief and leads to formal acceptance of his rule by the elders (1 Sam. 11) Since at this stage rule of the people is based on proven ability rather than hereditary assumption of the throne, Saul the war chief is certified as ruler only after a victory (11:14–15).

---

be analyzed as they are portrayed in the account of Saul becoming chief (see sidebar).

What this narrative makes clear are the forces that lead to unification. This is a survival strategy for the ancient Israelite tribes and their elders. However, also evident in the stories of David's rise to power (1 Sam. 16–2 Sam. 10) and the story of the division of the kingdom (1 Kings 11) is the tenuous nature of newly organized political units. Chiefdoms, based on the military and organizational acumen of their leaders, cannot cope with failure. Saul's weaknesses, portrayed quite graphically by an anti-Saulide narrator in 1 Samuel 13–15, make him unfit to rule and set the stage for his family's ouster from the throne. Similarly, Solomon's apostasy, building shrines for the gods of his many foreign wives (1 Kings 11:1–8), and the political ineptitude of his successor, Rehoboam (12:6–15), provide the opportunity for secession by the northern tribes. In fact, the tribal elders, who had invested a portion of their authority in Saul and David, were heavily suppressed by Solomon's introduction of a complex bureaucratic structure (4:1–28). Seeing an opportunity, they simply took back their endorsement from Rehoboam and transferred it to a new leader, Jeroboam (12:1–19), when it became clear that the central government was too weak to stop them.

What Can We Learn about Ancient Israel from the Social Institutions Described in the Biblical Narrative?

The investigation of the social institutions in ancient Israel is another major area of interest for social-scientific critics. These would include kinship patterns, concepts of honor and shame, gender roles, and patterns of association. At the heart of their studies is a blending of the older comparative methods of ethnographic analogy with materialist and ideological analysis. Strong emphasis is also placed on human experience as a generator of cultural patterns and customs.

Since the ancient Near East is not a living culture, much of the data for this type of analysis has to come from textual and artifactual evidence. We can draw on the emic interpretations of ancient cultures as long as we recognize that it is not always a true reflection of the social context of the biblical narrative or ancient Near Eastern records. Careful use of analogous data from the study of preindustrial cultures in the Middle East as well as modern tribal groups also has proven useful. For instance, obligations placed upon daughters to remain virginal prior to marriage and chaste after marriage as well as the obvious social and legal concerns over adultery are found in both the biblical and the ancient Near Eastern law codes and in the customary practices of Middle Eastern cultures (Matthews 1998). The question that has to be asked, however, is whether these social norms reflect the time period portrayed in the story or legal text or whether they are products of a later period that wishes to use the authority of the ancestral period to bolster their own interpretation of cultural mandates.

Recent studies of social customs in the Bible (Donaldson 1981; Steinberg 1993) make it clear that some of what appears in the biblical narratives and in legal materials contains ideal patterns and may not reflect lived reality. To be sure, there are examples in the text where the rules of society have to be set aside in the face of realities like childlessness, political dislocation due to immigration, and shifts in available or eligible marriage partners. In order to make this somewhat clearer, I will briefly discuss some of these social institutions and the sociological terminology that applies to them.

Gender Roles and Marriage Patterns

The examination of gender roles as described in the biblical text, applying the principles of ethnoarchaeology as well as economic models, has demonstrated that in the labor-intensive village culture, the small population relied upon the contributions of every person, male or female (Meyers 1988). Women worked hard alongside their husbands, brothers, and sons, both in the fields and as childbearers and managers of the household's resources (see an Egyptian attestation of the female role within the household in Matthews and Benjamin 2006: 226). However, they did not have the right to own land, could not serve in the assembly of elders, or, unlike in Mesopotamia, perform the role of priest. Their role in the domestic economy is emphasized in the narratives and provides them with status within the household. In addi-

147

Sociological Terms

Endogamy   The custom of marrying only within a defined group is illustrated by Abraham instructing his servant to find a bride for Isaac from "my kindred" rather than the "daughters of the Canaanites" (Gen. 24:3–4). This practice preserves cultural identity and ensures that the children are educated/socialized according to the group's own values and customs. However, the only points in the Bible where it is explicitly demanded of the Israelites are in the ancestral narratives and in the postexilic community of Yehud (Ezra 9–10; Neh. 13:23–27). In both instances, endogamy functions as a cultural survival strategy.

Exogamy   The custom of marrying outside one's own group was practiced by the Israelites (Num. 25:6; Ezra 10:2) but condemned as a source of religious and cultural contamination (Num. 25:7–8; Ezra 9:1–4). Marrying out has the economic advantage of obtaining inheritance rights to land or improving one's social status. For royalty, exogamy is also a means of establishing political alliances (e.g., Solomon's foreign wives in 1 Kings 3:1; 11:1–8).

Taboos   Every society demands certain behaviors and prohibits or taboos others. For example, all cultures establish codes that set standards for choosing sexual partners. Incest taboos further qualify these restrictions by forbidding sexual contact between close blood kin (brother, sister, mother, father). While this may be based on an understanding of the genetic problems caused by inbreeding, it also is concerned with inheritance patterns and matters of ritual purity (an extensive list of incest restrictions in Lev. 18 reflects the religious and social values of the postexilic priestly community). Incest taboos are sometimes ignored or set aside for royalty (e.g., David's children Amnon and Tamar in 2 Sam. 13:11–13).

Chastity codes   In the ancient Near East, female sexuality was an economic and social concern of fathers and husbands (see the Mesopotamian law codes: Code of Hammurapi 129–32, 155–57; Middle Assyrian Law 14–21). The standard in ancient Israelite society condemned any suspected or real violation of proper sexual conduct by women and punished men only when they were caught in the act of adultery or rape. At issue and as codified in the Ten Commandments (Exod. 20:14) is the value attached to a woman's ability to provide an heir for her husband and the assurance that her husband is the father of her children.

tion, there is evidence of female participation in mourning practices and victory celebrations as musicians and dancers (Meyers 1991).

Given the patriarchal nature of their society, it is therefore not surprising to find that arranged marriages were standard procedure in the ancient Near East for young women who were still members of their household (Matthews 2003b: 6–14). This varies, as might be expected, for widows and for women unassociated with a household. The biblical narrative includes a large number of instances in which marriage customs are an integral part of the story. Marriage, and especially the control of female sexuality, is spelled out in the legal codes. Sociological terms may be illustrated with references to specific biblical narratives.

INHERITANCE CUSTOMS

The national identity of the Israelites is intimately entwined with the Promised Land. The covenant promise made to Abram (Gen. 12:1–3; 15:18–21; 17:6–8) and renewed in the time of Moses (Exod. 19:3–6; 24:3–8) stipulates that

---

Violations of Sexual Custom

Exodus 22:16–17 and Deuteronomy 22:28–29 illustrate the value attached to virginity. An unmarried girl was the property of her father or head of household, and marriages were arranged to benefit the household economy. If the right of the father was usurped either by rape or consensual intercourse the girl's value as a bride was diminished, the household was shamed, and the father could be accused of failing to protect the household's assets. The laws in these texts protect the household's rights and provide restitution, a "virgin's bride price," so that the household is fully compensated and a measure of their honor is restored (compare Code of Hammurapi 130).

Numbers 5:11–31 deals with a married woman who has come under suspicion of infidelity (compare Code of Hammurapi 129). At the heart of this scenario is the right of the husband to demand that his wife prove her innocence (compare the new bride in Deut. 22:13–21). In this patriarchal society, the rights of the husband to control his wife's sexuality are most important. Even if she is only accused or a rumor has been spread, his honor is at risk, and this could have a ripple effect on his ability to engage in normal commerce in the community. Thus her word is not enough, and she is forced to take an oath and to undergo a physical ordeal, drinking a potion concocted by the priest. The assumption is that God will determine the outcome, and her only compensation, if proven innocent, is that her husband will be free of further shame.

Inheritance Terms

Patrilineal (or agnatic)   According to this social pattern, descent is passed through the male line from a founding father. Property is held by the male line and is passed exclusively to sons (either blood heirs or adopted males; Gen. 15:2). This concept initially explains the repeated references to the ancestral figures Abraham, Isaac, and Jacob (Exod. 3:15–16; 6:8; Deut. 1:8; 2 Kings 13:23), the tribal identities created by the households claiming to be descendants of Jacob's twelve sons (see the census in Num. 1:5–15), and the genealogies embedded in the text that certify lineage and the social status that goes with it (Num. 3:14–37; Ezra 2:1–57). Illegitimate sons could not receive an inheritance or claim a lineage unless the father made legal provision for this (see Jephthah's expulsion in Judg. 11:2; compare Middle Assyrian Law A.45, in Matthews and Benjamin 2006: 127).

Primogeniture   This inheritance pattern assigns the majority of the bequest to the oldest surviving son. This decision is based on there being a limit to the amount of land available to the Israelites in Canaan. Rather than divide up the land equally among all surviving sons and cut it into ever decreasing, economically infeasible pieces, a double portion was assigned to the oldest surviving son, and the rest received much smaller portions of their father's property (not necessarily including land). This concept of a double portion as principal heir also appears in terms of social status. Elisha requests that Elijah give him a "double share of your spirit" as evidence of his role as the prophet's heir (2 Kings 2:9).

Levirate obligation   When a married man dies without producing an heir, it is the obligation of his brother to impregnate his brother's widow in order to produce an heir for the dead man (Gen. 38:1–11; compare Hittite Law Code 193, in Matthews and Benjamin 2006: 118). However, this also means that the brother, who serves as levir, will not be able to inherit his brother's portion of their father's estate. This explains why Judah's son refuses to impregnate the widow Tamar: he wants to increase his own potential legacy. The legal loophole in Deuteronomy 25:5–10 that allows the levir to publicly renounce his obligation to the widow and the brother's estate suggests that even being shamed is not sufficient deterrent to providing a competing heir.

God will provide the Israelites with both land and children in exchange for their obedience to God's command. For them to remain a part of the covenant community, they must carefully ensure that each household is assigned a portion of the land and that these households pass their rights to this property down through the generations (Josh. 13:8–32). When a household was in danger of extinction, the elders or the leadership of that day could assign temporary custodianship to a guardian or levir (the lands of Elimelech of Bethlehem in Ruth 4:1–4) or to daughters until they married (Zelophehad's household in Num. 27:1–11; 36:2–12). If a household was utterly destroyed by war or by violation of the law, the monarchy took custody of the land so that it was not lost to the people of the covenant (1 Kings 21:15–16).

And, although the people are carried into exile for generations (597–535 BCE), the prophetic assurance given to them is that their claim to the land remains in effect as long as they remain faithful and cleanse themselves of the idolatry and other sins that had forced God to separate them from the land (see Jeremiah's redemption of family property in Jer. 32:1–15 and the exilic voice of Isaiah calling on the exiles to return and reclaim Zion in Isa. 40:1–11). Underlying this basic identity framework for ancient Israel are legal principles upon which inheritance within kinship groups was governed. They were based on the biblical narrative describing ancient Israel as a patrilineal society that chose to control the portioning out of property by granting the majority share to the eldest surviving son.

Patterns of Association

Social concepts such as reciprocity are often created as a means of social control (Matthews and Benjamin 1993: 121–22). Reciprocity in all of its forms functions as a balancing principle ensuring that every act has a social and/or legal consequence. As a result, gift-giving (kin-based and non-kin-based), hospitality, social welfare systems, and patron-client associations operate according to a recognized protocol within a culture. An imbalance can occur, however, if one party abuses the practice or disregards standard behavior (i.e., commits a crime).

Types of Reciprocity
(adapted from Sahlins 1972 and Stansell 1999)

Generalized reciprocity   Charity, hospitality, gifts given to kin and the circle of friends, in no instance requiring or expecting immediate return or service in exchange. In Genesis 18:1–8 Abraham provides hospitality to three strangers. He obtains honor from carrying out this social protocol correctly, and his guests are not expected to provide him with an immediate, balanced exchange of services. However, the assumption is that if Abraham were in a similar situation, he could expect to receive hospitality in turn. Charity is a form of gift-giving, but it does not carry with it an expectation of return and instead serves as a form of honorable, moral behavior. In the third century BCE, Ben Sirach goes so far as to state that a person should "show a cheerful face" when giving a gift since the Lord "will repay you sevenfold" (Sirach 35:11–13).

Balanced reciprocity   Exchange of gifts of equal value with little or no delay as part of the process of building social or political relationships. The assumption here is that unbalanced exchange can create measurable tensions. David protected the flocks of Nabal and asked that he receive food for his men in return. Nabal, an ally of Saul, refuses and insults David. David must redeem his honor by attacking Nabal's household but is assuaged when Nabal's wife, Abigail, presents David with the proper offering of food, thereby closing the circle of exchange (1 Sam. 25:2–35).

Imbalanced reciprocity   An aggressive tactic designed to shame someone by giving a gift they cannot financially or socially balance. It is used to intimidate or bribe an opponent. For example, Jacob gives his brother Esau a series of valuable gifts (Gen. 32:3–21) and then begs that Esau not give him anything in exchange—signally a peace offering. Restitution may be sought here to balance the earlier instance in which Jacob purchases Esau's birthright and as a means of obtaining honor while Esau contents himself with removal from Canaan to Edom (33:1–17).

Negative reciprocity   An aggressive tactic designed to obtain a greater return or even to get something for nothing through barter or theft. Abraham, a resident alien in the vicinity of Hebron, must haggle from a weak social position with Ephron the Hittite to purchase a burial cave. Ephron uses tactics that result in Abraham paying an exorbitant price (Gen. 23:7–16). Similarly, Absalom organizes a coup d'état and ousts David from the throne rather than wait for his father to die and inherit the kingdom as his heir (2 Sam. 15:1–18).

In addition to gift-giving, reciprocity governs legal principles such as *lex talionis* ("eye for an eye") clauses in ancient law (Exod. 21:24; Lev. 24:20; Code of Hammurapi 195–99, in Matthews and Benjamin 2006: 111–12). Although it is unlikely that anyone was actually expected to pluck out an eye as recompense for an injury, the issue is in fact the payment of damages equal to the value of the loss. Liability is central to this legal concept. For example, a dispute that results in one party being injured and missing work must be compensated to the value of any medical services necessary to recovery and for "the loss of time" (Exod. 21:18–19). In this way the balance and general harmony of the community can be restored.

The sense of mutual obligation that is implicit in biblical law is also found in the statutes that provide for the protected classes (e.g., widows, orphans, and strangers). Since these individuals lack the means to either feed or protect themselves in the same manner as normally connected persons or citizens, the entire community is obligated to render them assistance (e.g., gleaning in the fields; Deut. 24:19–22). In this way, no one is left entirely destitute, and no one is utterly estranged from legal protections (see the inclusion of "strangers" in the Sabbath laws in Exod. 20:10).

PATRON/CLIENT RELATIONS

Only utopian societies consist of members who have equal rights and who share everything in common without privilege or complaint. In the real world, differences between classes of people based on status, wealth, power, and kinship always separate people into hierarchies and provide clarity to social relationships. While an ordered society must provide a means of solving problems that arise between the classes, not everyone will receive exactly the same level of justice. Kinship obligations or loyalties help to solve many local disputes since the members of a household, clan, or tribe recognize that their actions have a direct consequence on the honor

153

or shame attached to the larger kinship group. However, the natural desire for preeminence may bring households or larger groups into conflict, and this provides opportunities for the creation of new leaders or a shift in the hierarchy of the most important lineages.

In the midst of the competition between kinship groups is the political reality that there are always going to be persons and groups who, based on their wealth or influence, can demand special preferment. There will also be those, because they lack influence, who will either have to live with disappointment or seek out the more powerful to assist them. One factor that works to the benefit of both classes of people is the desire of those who rise to leadership positions (elders and kings) to reinforce their status by obtaining the support of the rest of the community. This requirement of reaffirmation complements the reciprocal need of the common people to seek legal redress, protection of property, and guidance in times of crisis. It also places an obligation on leaders to care for the needs of their people.

The patron-client relationship as it appears in the biblical narrative is a social response to the needs of both of these parties. The patron, often referred to by the kinship term *father*, functions in much the same way as the head of a household but with more authority and with the ability to redistribute greater resources. Their "sons" are more than just subordinates (see Elijah and Elisha in 2 Kings 2:12). They provide services to their patron in the form of work (manual or civic), military duties as needed, and public respect. In this way, the patron who is esteemed by society provides justice, employment, food, and protection and thereby obtains greater honor within the community and is able to extend his authority to a wider network of clients.

Patron-client arrangements are less formal than covenant agreements. They simply require someone of lesser authority or means to accept the assistance or gift of a person of great authority and wealth (Crook 2006: 86). Covenantal

---

Patron-Client Relationships

Individual patron   When a person's wealth and influence makes it possible to draw both kin and nonkin under his umbrella of care and protection, potential clients will seek him out in order to create an association. Ruth, who has no social standing in Bethlehem except by extension from her widowed mother-in-law, requests that Boaz recognize her as one of his "servants" (Ruth 2:10–13) and later pleads for his intercession in the dispute over her father-in-law's property (3:9–10). He subsequently takes her case to the elders, assuming the role of patron and later of husband (4:1–12).

Village or city elders   Persons recognized as coming from the most influential lineages are considered to be wise and responsible and are property owners (T. Willis 2001: 9–12). They sit in the gate and listen to testimony and then speak from the consensus of law and community tradition on the cases brought before them. Thus the slandered virgin's case is brought to the elders at the gate, evidence is presented by her parents, and once her innocence is determined the elders impose a fine on the husband who brought the accusation (Deut. 22:13–19). The patrons/elders prevent conflict from escalating between two households by hearing this case and making a ruling that removes potential harm to both. This then adds to the elders' honor and authority.

King   By its nature a government is too complex for a single individual to manage all of its affairs. A bureaucracy is created to deal with the minutia of administration while the king provides overall leadership. The patronage system that fills the offices of the bureaucracy is a major tool employed by kings to reward friends and kin, recognize merit, and create alliances with supporters throughout the kingdom. Saul initially installs his own kin in these positions (nepotism), but Solomon's clients apparently come from a larger pool (1 Kings 4:1–19). David also employs foreign mercenaries (Uriah the Hittite, Ittai the Gittite) in his military and his palace guard, an indication that patronage extends beyond national boundaries when it serves the purpose of the patron.

---

agreements are by their nature more formal, involving strict rituals and a detailed expression of terms (especially in treaty language). These higher level contractual arrangements are made between nations in the form of suzerain treaties and parity treaties (equal partners). The former transforms a sovereign nation that had previously operated without obligations to other states into a vassal nation, in essence a client of a larger, more powerful state or empire. For instance, during the eighth and much of the seventh century BCE, Israel and Judah were vassals of the Assyrian Empire. They paid tribute, supplied troops for the Assyrian war machine, and swore loyalty to the rulers of Assyria in exchange for protection against their enemies (2 Kings 15:19–20, 29). While the biblical account is not always as explicit about these political ties as one might hope, there are a few instances where a king makes it very clear who his master/patron is. Thus, when King Ahaz of Judah is threatened by his neighbors, he sends a "gift" and a plea to Tiglath-pileser III of Assyria, saying, "I am your servant and your son. Come up, and rescue me from the hand of the king of Aram and from the hand of the king of Israel, who are attacking me" (16:7–8). Assyria responds by invading the region and capturing Damascus. In essence, Ahaz's safety comes at the expense of other Assyrian vassals that had become delinquent (16:9).

ISRAEL'S COVENANT RELATIONSHIP WITH YAHWEH

The relationship between Israel and Yahweh is expressed in anthropomorphic terms. Humans tend to consider their behavior to be an imitation (mimesis) of divine behavior and therefore describe their divine patrons as if they were human. Thus when God chooses to create this association, terms of the contractual arrangement are set in much the same way as a suzerain treaty between two nations: in exchange for land and children (i.e., forms of fertility), the people of Israel are required to limit their devotion to Yahweh alone and to obey his commandments. Additional benefits of this gift of God include protection from their enemies, with the aid of the Divine Warrior (Exod. 17:8–16), the nurturing assistance of a father to widows and orphans (Ps. 68:5–6), and general prosperity resulting from God's control over the forces of nature (Isa. 30:23–26; Zech. 10:1). It would be impossible for the Israelites to repay God for the gift of the covenant, and therefore the only way in which they can demonstrate

Covenant Statements

The covenant statements in Israelite tradition all speak to the promise of land and children in exchange for complete obedience and devotion to Yahweh. They also, in their various ways, create a covenantal theology that ultimately, by the time of the postexilic period (after 500 BCE), makes the case for monotheism in a world where polytheism is the norm.

Genesis 17:2–14 The most elaborate of three covenant statements made to Abram/Abraham (see also Gen. 12:1–3; 15:5–7) includes the command to be "blameless" (i.e., obedient) and to circumcise all males, as well as a promise of many descendants, continuance of the covenant through the generations, "all the land of Canaan," and a name change. The responsibility of the human covenant partners is that "I will be their God."

Exodus 19:4–6 A capsule summary of the covenant bond following the exodus from Egypt now includes a phrase that will become a refrain when the covenant is mentioned: "You have seen what I did to the Egyptians, and how I bore you on eagles' wings and brought you to myself" (see Exod. 20:2; Judg. 2:1; Hos. 11:1). The people are then commanded to "obey my voice and keep my covenant," and they will in turn be God's "treasured possession" and "a priestly kingdom and a holy nation" (setting them on a higher standard than other peoples).

Deuteronomy 6:1–9 The exhortation to keep God's decrees and commandments takes the form of a promise "so that you may multiply greatly in a land flowing with milk and honey." Then the Shema/statement of faith is provided for them to recite to their children, bind on their hands and forehead (this is the origin of phylacteries), and affix to their doorposts (in a mezuzah): "The Lord is our God, the Lord alone. You shall love the Lord your God with all your heart, and with all your soul, and with all your might" (6:4–5).

Jeremiah 7:22–26 Since the covenant with Yahweh is an example of unbalanced reciprocity, attempts were made by the Israelites to create rituals and perform sacrifices (elements of worship common to neighboring religions) that could demonstrate devotion and perhaps even balance the gifts of the covenant. This belief or strategy is repeatedly rejected by the Hebrew prophets (Hos. 6:6; Amos 5:21–24). Jeremiah notes that when God rescued them from Egypt he "did not speak to them or command them concerning burnt offerings and sacrifices" (Jer. 7:22). Instead the essence of the covenant is: "Obey my voice, and I will be your God, and you shall be my people; and walk only in the way that I command you, so that it may be well with you" (7:23).

their submission to its terms is to be obedient and to show their fidelity to God by abstaining from the worship of any other gods (Exod. 20:3).

This reciprocal agreement is implicitly based on the continuous faithfulness of Israel. Thus failure to uphold the terms of the agreement has its downside. As an indignant patron punishes an unfaithful client, God will withhold the benefits of the covenant by suppressing the rains and allowing the harvests to shrink (Jer. 3:3; Hag. 1:6). In the end, when it becomes clear that the Israelites will not listen to these divine warnings (Jer. 7:24–26), God will allow them to be conquered by foreign nations (Isa. 5:24–30) and returned to the "wilderness" of the exile until such time as they are purified and prepared to be obedient (Isa. 40:1–2; Ezek. 36:26).

Concluding Statement

Given the limitations of archaeology and the growing body of social-scientific methods being developed to analyze modern cultures, it is appropriate to utilize these methods in the service of our study of ancient Israel. While it must be understood that these techniques also have their limitations and must be used carefully so that they do not predetermine the social reconstruction of elements found through "excavating" ancient sites and the biblical text, their usefulness has been proven over the past three decades. Together with literary approaches and the data supplied by examination of the material remains of ancient Israel, a social-world reading of the text provides new insights and a better sense of the lives portrayed in the biblical narratives and other ancient Near Eastern texts.

5

History and Historiography

W hat are the sources that contribute to the creation of a history of ancient Israel and Judah?

History is more than something that happened once upon a time. Before we concern ourselves with the past, our own or that of the ancient Israelites, we will have to examine why we choose to be concerned. If there is a true benefit to be derived from the exercise, it must be more than simple curiosity. The exploration of history and history writing says a great deal about who we are and who we wish to be. In fact, history provides a frame of reference upon which to build personal and national identity. It adds authority to government policies and religious ideologies. To refine this, a recent definition of history describes it as "a story the present tells itself about the past, and its meaning lies in the interaction of the two" (Hedrick 2006: 1). And, whether the history we tell is based on our perception of "the facts" or is invented to justify a current social or political agenda, it generally satisfies our need to know our origins—at least, until a new

159

movement arises that again wishes to begin the process over and reexamine the records.

While the history of any nation includes a series of events and dates, that is far from the whole story. History consists of a sequence of events that are considered significant enough to the people involved or to their descendants to be remembered, recited, and recorded. When no one remembers these events, then that portion of the history of the world is lost until a historian uncovers the records and artifacts that have survived and attempts to recreate at least a portion of that lost history. In this way, some of what has been forgotten about the world of ancient Israel has been brought to light through the work of historians who have made use of the biblical text, ancient Near Eastern documents, the artifactual remains uncovered by archaeologists, and the social theories developed by sociologists and anthropologists. However, it is not enough to want to retell a story that was lost or whose meaning has become hazy to modern readers. The historian must strive to tell "the most likely story" in order to "account for the reality of what happened in the past" (Barstad 1997: 44).

If the principal aim of this final chapter was to provide a basic orientation to the history of ancient Israel, I would chronicle the origins of the people, their political development from a group of loosely affiliated tribes into a chiefdom and eventually into a kingdom, and their relations with other nations. This would require me to provide an array of dates, events, and personal names, and it is quite likely that my presentation would confirm the long-held aversion of many students to reading history textbooks. In fact, I do intend to provide some of this information, but it is not my primary focus here, and I will leave that task to those who have written a formal history of Israel (see the list at the end of this chapter). Instead, what I want to concentrate on is (1) the process that led to the composition of the history of Israel by the Israelites themselves and (2) how modern historians interpret that writing process and the various sources available to us about the world of ancient Israel.

It is virtually impossible to write a completely objective history because of the social filtering that has taken place both at the point when historical records were first produced and at each point when these records were reviewed and pieced together into what is considered a coherent "history" of related events. Special care must be taken to ensure that the historian is at least aware of the forces that will influence and can complicate the process of working with historical records, since "he cannot do his work at all without assumptions and judgments" (Finley 1975: 61). As a result, when examining ancient sources, modern historians have to learn to recognize and take into account such things as self-serving propaganda, theological justifications for the decisions that were made in the editing process, and the culture-centered masking of real intentions. After this, one

---

Methodological Considerations

- Historians examine primary sources: legends, prayers, official accounts, as well as economic, administrative, political, and legal records.
- Historians examine not only written sources but also material remains recovered by archaeologists and ethnographies compiled by anthropologists.
- Historians recognize that storytellers were not objective. They wanted their audience to know what their experiences meant for their lives. They were not describing what happened, but what it meant. In doing this they were selective in describing the events contained in their story.
- Historians recognize that any history of an ancient culture is always incomplete and subject to reinterpretation.
- Historians cannot completely set aside the influences of their own society or acquired political and ideological views.
- Historians tell the stories not only of the lives of the rich and famous but also of the poor and anonymous.
- Historians tell the stories not only of men but also of women.
- Historians tell the stories not only of what humans have done but also of how the earth has developed.

---

can then analyze the reasons why this material so often contains a programmed, agenda-based viewpoint on events. During the course of our study, we therefore will explore the current scholarly dialogue on writing a history of Israel, examine the tools employed by historians, and discuss the types of data that they use to make their case using a set of methodological considerations (see sidebar).

Semiotics of History

Philosopher Charles Pierce, as part of his 1906 essay entitled "Pragmatism in Retrospect: A Last Formulation," suggested a means of creating a semiotics of history (Buchler 1955: 269–79). Semiotics includes the study of how meaning is created and understood. By applying this method it is possible to see historical sources as reflective of both the "writer's interpretation of history" and as something that affects a reader when studying a historical record (Laato 2005: 166–67). One way to illustrate this is in the form of a double triad, linear diagram:

object → interpreter → sign → interpretant → affectant → second sign

This string of terms represents the following:

- **object**—the original event that has occurred (e.g., a battle, a coronation)
- **interpreter**—an eyewitness who chooses to memorialize the event by either telling about it or composing a written account
- **sign**—the record of the event (either oral or written) created by the interpreter
- **interpretant**—the full range of possible meanings that could be drawn about the record of the event based on culturally understood norms of behavior

162

- **affectant**—a person affected by hearing or reading the record and able to draw a recognizable set of meanings from the received record
- **second sign**—a second-level record of the event that has now been filtered through a secondary process of analysis based on the affectant's understood range of meanings for the interpretant

The recording and interpretation of history is therefore like the continually expanding ripples on a pond created by a pebble's original impact with the water. It is a continuous, dynamic process for every new affectant (i.e., historian or student) who examines either the original sign or any subsequent sign and produces yet another sign when a new history of the event is produced. In other words, history is continuously reinterpreted and shaped based on a never-ending sequence of creating records, examining records, and creating new records.

Having said this, however, it must also be admitted that we must take into account the social context or "referential world" of every interpreter from the very beginning of the string. The first interpreter is an eyewitness who makes the choice to create the first sign or record. This may be something as simple as telling a neighbor about the event or, as we will see below, placing a seal impression on a storage jar. However, the sign that the interpreter creates contains only that portion of the original event that he or she wishes to include or in fact understands or remembers. In other words, a filtering process occurs at the earliest stages of the process, and this contributes to the number of possible meanings or social understandings contained in the interpretant of the record that has been produced.

In order to gain a better understanding of how this may have worked in antiquity, we will now examine a variety of examples of the recording and interpretative process. Each example will speak to a particular type of record, and

163

each in turn will allow us to discuss how that record can be interpreted based on whether the interpreter shares the referential world of the originator of the record or is from another era entirely.

Record Keeping in the Palace at Mari

The cuneiform archives recovered from the ancient northern Mesopotamian city of Mari (dating to 1800–1750 BCE) deal with a variety of administrative topics, including many economic documents that record everyday activities of the palace workers and scribes. They also include official accounts of the transactions made with vendors and an exact list of all daily distributions of supplies, clothing, and food by the palace. A parallel to these procedures is found in the accounting in 1 Kings 4:22–23 of the provision of food served in Solomon's palace. Both the Mari texts and the biblical account include a detailed description of the amount and type of food prepared for the meals that were served every day in their respective palace complexes. In the Mari texts, the original accounting of meals for any particular day was kept on a single cuneiform tablet and then stored for later use. However, this was sometimes a rather haphazard process since the tablets were not stored in alphabetic order or even placed in the same archive room in the palace that housed similar texts. The further discovery that monthly ledger tablets were created indicates that at some later date another scribe gathered all of the information placed on these single-day accounts into a monthly log that allowed the palace administrator to get a sense not only of the amounts of food being prepared but also of the total costs involved.

The trouble with this procedure is that the apparently inefficient manner in which the original tablets were stored made it difficult for the second scribe to gather all of the relevant texts for his ledger entries. In addition, the level

164

Writing a Cuneiform tablet (Courtesy of Zev Radovan)

of training of the scribes was not always the same, and that contributed to spelling inconsistencies, illegible texts, and mathematical errors. Examination of these ledger texts has shown some discrepancies that may be accounted for by (1) a scribe simply using data from an available text rather than the original for that day when he could not locate the needed document or (2) intentional doctoring of the books to hide embezzlement or inefficiency (Sasson 1982: 239–41). That scribes were not above suspicion is demonstrated in a letter (Archives royales de Mari 10.90) implicating a high-ranking administrator for embezzlement (compare the financing problems associated with the repair of the temple in 2 Kings 12:4–16). However, in this case, the decision was made to require the dishonest administrator only to pay a fine because his skills as a trained scribe and manager were too valuable to lose (Matthews 2002b: 171).

Applying our model of historical semiotics to the Mari example, the original interpreter of the event is the first scribe who observes the actual preparation or delivery of meals and then records that fact on his cuneiform tablet. The second scribe is the affectant who later consults the original record and draws the data from that text to create his second sign, the monthly ledger of expenses. However, the second scribe

165

may choose to alter the data he finds on the original text to fit his own plans (embezzlement?) or may draw data from another text if he cannot locate the cuneiform tablet for the day in question. That is where the interpretant or possible set of meanings supplied by the sign comes into this process. The second scribe may judge that the figures recorded on the original tablet are incorrect (a mathematical error may be evident) or that the items listed may be so unusual that they are questionable in the normal course of food preparation. In any case, it is not always just a simple transfer of data from one text to another. There is always going to be a decision-making process employed by the second scribe when he creates his second sign to either record the information exactly as he reads it or to make alterations. And, of course, he may make an error in the copying process that will alter subsequent use of the data.

In this case, the affectant (second-level interpreter) shares the referential world of the original interpreter. He is a contemporary, living in the royal palace complex, has had similar training, and is assigned to a task very similar to that of the first scribe. Even so, this does not ensure that the original record will remain intact. Factors that contribute to change include the ability to deal with the realities of inefficiency that exist in the record-keeping process, the relative skills of both scribes, and the possibility for fraud and dishonesty implicit in any situation involving large quantities of goods.

Israelite Administrative Practices and the *lmlk* Seal Impressions

Unfortunately, we have not as yet uncovered an archive of Israelite administrative documents such as that found at the site of ancient Mari. This is not to say that there are no clues about government policies, but they are not on the same scale as the hundreds of cuneiform documents available to historians of ancient Mesopotamia. What archaeologists have discovered in their excavations of Israelite cities is indirect evidence of administrative practices that can be coupled with details contained in the royal annals recorded in the Bible. For example, in 2 Chronicles 32:27–28, the "great riches and honor" associated with the reign of Hezekiah of Judah are demonstrated by a list of his treasures (silver, gold, precious stones, spices, shields, etc.). In addition, the king is said to have built storehouses for grain, wine, and oil, stalls for cattle, and sheepfolds. The phrase *riches and honor* is applied to other well-esteemed kings of Israel and Judah, including Solomon (1 Kings 3:13) and Jehoshaphat (2 Chron. 17:5), and both of these kings are said to have built storehouse cities (1 Kings 9:19; 2 Chron. 17:12).

Gedaliah seal

It is quite likely that the management of all these resources was put into the hands of scribes and overseers, who served the kings as the heart of the royal bureaucracy. Among the objects that archaeologists have recovered that provide first-hand evidence of the tasks assigned to these individuals are personal seals and their impressions. For example, the seal depicted in the nearby illustration, which was discovered at Lachish, contains the inscription "Gedaliah, who is over the house" and refers to a person who managed a royal estate (J. Graham 1984: 57). This rather mundane object might be compared to a modern rubber stamp or a notary's stamp that contains a name and office. It would have been created at the time the person was appointed to the position since it was personalized with his name and may have remained as a family heirloom after he left the office or died.

Even though five different persons from various time periods bear the name Gedaliah in the biblical text, it is not possible to tie any one of them to this particular stamp. It contains too little information for us to be able to unequivocally say that it is the property of a biblical personage. Its value in this case is to be found in how it points to social and economic organization in ancient Israel.

Having a personal object belonging to a person who served the royal house allows us to visualize his tasks and draw on references in the biblical record to the work of bureaucrats. One additional example among the many available is a seventh-century ovoid seal made of green quartz (15 millimeters x 11 millimeters) that has been dated based on its paleography (style of writing). It contains the name Pela'yahu (Pelaiah—a Levite bears this name in Neh. 8:7), and the accompanying inscription identifies him as having charge "over the corvée" (Avigad 1980: 170–71). Only one person holds this title in the biblical account, Adoram (2 Sam. 20:24; 1 Kings 12:18), who is said to have served both David and Solomon. However, the date of this seal provides an indication that both corvée (i.e., forced labor) and the office of the overseer continued to be part of government service in later periods. One additional social marker provided by this seal is the name of the official: Pela'yahu, which includes a form of the name of the Israelite God Yahweh. The practice of including theophoric (divine) elements in personal names is quite common in the ancient Near East, and in this case it is an indication that his family chose to express their faith in Yahweh by adding this element to his personal name.

Yet another example of the complexity of government service is found in the list of civic officials purported to serve David's need for trained administrators (1 Chron. 27:25–31). Most scholars doubt that David's government would have required such an extensive bureaucracy since the 2 Samuel account indicates that Israel was at that point a fledgling state just emerging from its confederation of tribal groups into a more cohesive chiefdom (Flanagan 1988: 251–52; Frick 1985: 202–3). Since there is no way to test the veracity of this list of David's officials and since it actually dates to a period at least five hundred years after David's reign (Japhet 1993: 470), the most that it can tell us is that complex administrative structures were known in ancient Israel (at least in the postexilic period). It is possible that bureaucratic hierarchies existed in many of the eras associated with the Israelite monarchy and functioned as part of a complex administrative system. But there is no way, using existing data, to draw the conclusion that this list is anything but a record artificially assigned to the reign of David. Its authenticity is based solely on the likelihood that as the government grew it required a larger set of officials to carry out the tasks of administration.

Having examined both archaeological and textual evidence of administrative practices, we can now combine these details with another physical record that dates to the reign of King Hezekiah of Judah in the latter part of the eighth century BCE. Physical evidence indicates that during his reign royal scribes differentiated jars of olive oil and wine that were the property of the king from those belonging to private individuals by applying a seal impression to the jar handle before it was fire hardened. These two-winged and four-winged impressions all contained the Hebrew phrase *lmlk* ("belonging to the king"). Many of the over 1,700 seal impressions discovered to date also include city or regional names (Hebron, Socoh, Ziph), which may indicate the origin of the jar or the area in which the wine or oil was produced. Although we have not found any of the seals themselves, the impressions that they made function in much the same way as those impressed into the bottom of plastic jars in modern stores to indicate the maker or distributor of a product.

Archaeological evidence, based on where the seal impressions have been found (specifically Level III at Lachish), comparative ceramic analysis of the shape and composition of the clay, and the examination of destruction levels associated with the Assyrian campaign in Judah of 701 BCE, indicates that these seal impressions were applied only during the reign of Hezekiah and apparently were not used by later kings (Ussishkin 1977; Vaughn 1999: 85–86). The few jars containing these seals that have been discovered in excavation levels dating to the seventh century may simply indicate that some of the eighth-century jars had survived the Assyrian invasion and continued to be used by subsequent inhabitants of sites in Judah (Mazar, Amit, and Ilan 1984: 248–50).

The range of interpretations for this practice of applying a distinctive seal impression to a particular set of storage jars includes the following: (1) evidence of taxation, (2) designation of rations for fortress sites on Judah's borders, (3) a part of the buildup program in the months prior to an expected Assyrian invasion of Judah to prepare for siege conditions, and (4) a general program of reform designed to bolster the economy of the nation and increase the influence of the monarchy over the entire country that was begun years before the threat of Assyrian reprisals (Vaughn 1999: 169–72). While any of these suggested interpretations are possible and could be considered valid, our model of historical investigation allows us to make only a probable conclusion while leaving the issue open enough to be able to adapt to any new information that may come to light.

As for the reasons why the *lmlk* seals were not used by later kings, we are faced once again with a range of possibilities. These could include outside pressure from Judah's political overlords, the kings of Assyria, to end a practice associated with a rebellious vassal ruler. It is also possible that the destruction of the cities where the seals were manufactured and applied was a factor in the abandonment of the practice.

When a new generation of scribes arose to serve the more compliant monarch, Manasseh (2 Kings 21:1–9), older policies could have been supplanted or set aside for a variety of reasons as the new king and his advisors were forced to accept closer supervision by the Assyrian overlords. However, without an explicit record explaining why the seals were no longer used, we can only speculate.

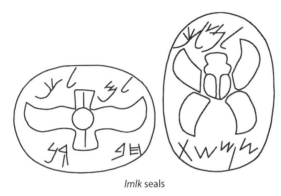

lmlk seals

What becomes clear in this example is the reduced percentage of possible interpretant meanings evident to the affectant when that person is separated by a gulf of time from the original event (the placing of the seal impression on the jars). An affectant (archaeologist or historian) living three thousand years after the original event occurs will not share the same social understandings or make the same assumptions about the event that an original interpreter or contemporary affectant (a scribe of Hezekiah's household) would have when viewing one of these seal impressions.

As a result, the modern affectant, such as an archaeologist who discovers one of these inscribed jars, is less likely to perceive or appreciate the full range of possible meanings. Every reaction to the sign (the seal impression) will have either a narrower interpretant range or one that may be foreign to the intention of the original interpreter. Based on these limitations, all we can safely say as modern affectants is (1) that the seal impressions exist, (2) that the jars upon which they exist can be dated (based on archaeological evidence) to a specific time period and a specific king of ancient Judah, and (3) that seals ceased to appear on jars associated with later kings of Judah. This information contributes in some ways to our reconstruction of events in ancient Judah, but it certainly does not answer all of our questions or tell us the full story of this intriguing administrative practice.

Sennacherib's 701 BCE Campaign

The vast cuneiform archives discovered in the royal palace at Nineveh contain the literature, economic documents, and royal annals of the kings of Assyria. Their written content is supplemented and visually reinforced by dozens of limestone and alabaster relief panels hung on the walls of that palace complex. These reliefs function as a visual form of propaganda and depict imperial policy and ideology. Both the written records and the official art of the Assyrian palace have provided historians with records of military campaigns, including those of King Sennacherib of Assyria, who invaded Judah in 701 BCE. They both depict how the bold King Sennacherib swiftly moved to pacify a potential or real revolt by his vassals in Syria-Palestine and in the process conquered or besieged a number of cities. However, they both are actually second signs, secondhand accounts that have been shaped into official accounts of a campaign by Assyrian scribes. As such, their reliability as a true recitation of events is questionable (Henige 2005: 45).

Assyrian Annals

Because the Assyrian annals are a narrative history and therefore subject to the royal ideological selection process fostered by the king and his advisors and implemented by the scribes

172

involved in the formulation of the end product, they cannot be considered to be objective renderings of events (Becking 2003: 51). Examination of the written accounts, with their long lists of battles in which well-equipped armies with siege engines are employed in the capture of rebel cities, demonstrates a scribal tradition or style that was used for the annals of many different Assyrian rulers (Younger 1990: 68). The enemy is always described as having brought this disaster upon themselves. The Assyrian ruler accuses them of having failed to "bow to my feet quickly (enough)" or to "submit to my yoke" (Pritchard 1969: 287). Furthermore, the Assyrian records stipulate that their rulers are justified in their aggressive actions because they are men "who love righteousness" and who act to preserve justice and end treachery, giving "aid to the destitute" and redressing wrongs (Oded 1992: 32–33).

It is quite plain in the Assyrian account that once Sennacherib's invasion has begun, the style of reporting turns to prideful boasts by the king. Every rebel will learn that resistance is futile, and each will fall victim to his "terror-inspiring splendor." Furthermore, they will pay for their disloyalty with the slaughter of their armies, the loss of vast quantities of loot and prisoners, and the imposition of heavier tribute payments on their successors. Adding to Assyrian prowess is the repeated declaration that the king has been aided in his exploits by the gods of Assyria, who in turn are demonstrating their role as "the great judge of heaven and earth" through a trial by combat (Oded 1992: 38–39).

What is not quite so standard in the report on Hezekiah and the siege of Jerusalem, however, is that the city was not captured and the king of Judah was not forced, like other monarchs, to come to the Assyrian ruler and kiss his feet (Hallo and Younger 1997–2002: 2.303 §119B). Apparently, some management of events was necessary so that the Assyrians retained their aura of invincibility without having to admit this had not been a complete victory. Among the measures employed is the exaggerated listing of 200,150 prisoners, which accompanied the standard chronicle of animals, chariots, and other items of value. Of course, even if Jerusalem did not fall, the countryside of Judah and most of its fortified cities were destroyed, and both accounts agree that Hezekiah emptied his treasury to satisfy the Assyrian ruler, who it is reported in the Assyrian annals had already returned to Nineveh (Gallagher 1999: 132–35). It may then be concluded that both the Assyrian account and 2 Kings 18–20 are based in part on records of the events of Sennacherib's campaign. However, neither should be considered a complete or objective version. Their similarities and the archaeological record (Ussishkin 1997a: 320–21) indicate that destruction levels at Judean cities date to 701 and that Judean control over its own countryside continued after that date. Their main value, however, lies in interpreting the history of that period (Becking 2003: 67–68).

Relief Panels in the Palace of Nineveh

In addition to the cuneiform record, a large number of carved alabaster and limestone relief panels hung in specifically selected rooms or hallways within the palace at Nineveh, contain depictions of many of the events in Sennacherib's campaign. While they supply visual representations of events described in the written annals of the king, these reliefs are not dependent upon a subtext behind the images. In fact they stand as a parallel narrative created by the storyteller (the king) and supply details about the scenes of battle, the topography, and the social signatures of clothing, armor, and weapons (Winter 1981: 2). As such, these pictorial representations should not be considered inferior to the written account. They are simply another means of communication (S. James 1997: 24–25).

As part of our discussion of these visual records, we will explore some of the standard questions asked by art historians when making reconstructions based on images (see sidebar). In the process we will affirm that "representation is never innocent" and that every image employs "technical devices, formal conventions, and ideological assumptions to orchestrate meaning" (Moser and Smiles 2005: 1). What is conveyed in a work of art such as the Assyrian reliefs is a filtered portion of reality. Realism may be limited by the medium (stone, plaster, wood), but the more important factor will be the intention (the referential world) of the artist and his patron/employer.

Questions Asked by Art Historians

- Who created the piece of art in question?
- Was it a personal expression or a commissioned piece of art?
- Where was it displayed originally and why there in particular?
- What can it tell us about politics, religion, gender, social customs, and styles of artistic expression in the period during which it was created?
- What methods and devices does it use to manipulate its viewers?

The questions that the art historian chooses to ask about a piece of artwork will influence the kind of data he or she will choose to collect in order to answer them, but it should be apparent that finding answers is not always an easy or straightforward process. And, since this is interpretative thinking, it will lead to the creation of a second sign.

The reliefs that decorate the palace are part of a scheme employed by a sequence of Assyrian rulers to impress visitors. Sennacherib makes this point in his annals, boasting that they are intended to evoke the "astonishment of all nations" (Luckenbill 1968: 177 §413). Moreover, they had been intentionally placed along the entranceway to the throne room and were designed to intimidate and unnerve visitors or the ambassadors of other nations who were able to come into the presence of the king. The overt message, as presented in a linear sequence of telescoped scenes within the panel, provides a selective representation of "reality" of these historical events and is quite unambiguous (Winter

175

1981: 18, 24–25). They are meant to convey to all who see them that the king is all powerful and that the ferocious Assyrian army can never be defeated by rebellious vassals (Jacoby 1991: 113).

Their placement within the palace may also speak to the growing desire on the part of the Assyrian rulers to create a unifying image for what had become a very diverse empire. As new peoples were conquered or forced into vassalage, the social diversity of the empire had become a problem. This had created tensions that could and eventually did tear this vast empire apart. By representing a "law and order" stance and portraying an image of invincibility in their reliefs, the Assyrian kings may have been attempting to create a sense of "shared need" for stability within an increasingly complex population. By spreading the "Assyrian social umbrella" over all of these peoples in artistic representations, they might be able to minimize the lack of the "collective consciousness" that usually holds together more homogenous groups. In this way, they might minimize further revolts or social unrest (Durkheim 1972: 145; Winter 1981: 30).

Cuneiform captions have also been added to reinforce the message of the images for literate viewers and to anchor elements within the images in their minds (Barthes 1977: 38). Specifically, strategically placed inscriptions in Sennacherib's reliefs identify the personages and events in each scene. For instance, below the figure of the king is inscribed the statement: "Sennacherib, king of the universe, king of Assyria, sat upon a chair (while) the booty of Lachish passed before him" (Luckenbill 1968: 198 §489).

It is unclear how the artists obtained their information to create this visual form of political rhetoric, which was produced not necessarily to depict exact events or places but for the effect it has on viewers. Even in their stylized and biased form, both the visual and written accounts include information on the capture of the important border town of Lachish and the deportation of some of its surviving population and of the subsequent siege of Jerusalem in 701 BCE. However, none of these second signs purports to be the eyewitness accounts of soldiers who participated in the fighting. They are in fact official accounts, very likely written or depicted primarily for their propaganda value, and were produced by interpreters of oral or possibly written reports by persons involved in the events. What this means is that we lack the original sign or account of the battles and must work from ancient sources that are interpretations with specific agendas rather than from firsthand accounts.

Judahite refugees

The value of the Assyrian accounts, both written and visual, for a reconstruction of Israelite history is found in their (1) contribution to the establishment of a chronological anchor for dates assigned by historians to other biblical events and the reigns of monarchs in Israel and Judah and (2) independent corroboration of some events in the biblical narrative (e.g., 2 Kings 18–20) (Edelman 2000: 90–91; Becking 2003: 52–60). This is not to say that the Assyrian version is any more historical than the biblical narrative. Both are second-sign versions, and both contain a selective interpretative viewpoint on the events involved in Sennacherib's campaign.

Naturally, the perspective on events in the Assyrian annals stands in rather stark contrast to that found in the biblical text. Sennacherib's annals are a continuous tribute to his suppression of rebellious vassals and victories over his chief rival, the Egyptians. He does give credit to his patron god, Ashur, whose terrifying weapons allowed the king to overwhelm the fortified cities of Phoenicia, Philistia, Amurru (Moab, Edom), and Judah. The biblical account, dependent for its character on the ideological perspective on these events of the sixth-century Deuteronomistic Historian (see chapter 3), puts as positive a face as possible on Hezekiah's reforms, including a renovation and cleansing of the Jerusalem temple (2 Kings 18:3–7a), but does not mask the disastrous effects of the king's rebellion against Assyria. Archaeological evidence points to Hezekiah's political challenge to Assyrian rule leading to the devastation of Judah's cities and its economy, but there is no evidence at this point of an Assyrian siege of Jerusalem (Grabbe 2003: 6–20). Both the Assyrian account and 2 Kings describe how the king of Judah is forced to strip the nation of its riches, including those in the temple and palace, to pay a ransom for the city of Jerusalem (2 Kings 18:13–16). Like the Assyrian god, Ashur, Judah's god also plays a role in the drama (2 Kings 19). The Deuteronomistic Historian describes how a penitent king Hezekiah consults the prophet Isaiah and is assured that the Assyrian king will be drawn away by divinely inspired political rumors and that the city will be spared (19:5–7, 32–34).

Sennacherib's Campaign in 701 BCE (Hallo and Younger 1997–2002: 2.303 §119B)	Biblical Record of Sennacherib's Invasion (2 Kings 18)
Hezekiah is mentioned several times in conjunction with the rebellion of the Philistines, and Judah's cities are besieged and captured. He is said to have "not submitted to my yoke" in the Cylinder C version of the text (Gallagher 1999: 129).	Hezekiah "rebelled against the king of Assyria and would not serve him" (18:7b).

Sennacherib's Campaign in 701 BCE (Hallo and Younger 1997–2002: 2.303 §119B)	Biblical Record of Sennacherib's Invasion (2 Kings 18)
Sennacherib notes that the people of Ekron had deposed their king, Padi, and handed him over in fetters to Hezekiah the Judean. After defeating an army of Egyptians that had supported Ekron, Sennacherib freed Padi from Jerusalem and imposed tribute.	Hezekiah "attacked the Philistines as far as Gaza and its territory" (18:8). Hezekiah sends a message to Sennacherib at Lachish: "I have done wrong; withdraw from me; whatever you impose on me I will bear" (18:14).
"I besieged forty-six of his [Hezekiah's] fortified walled cities and surrounding smaller towns." "I took out 200,150 people . . . , horses, mules, donkeys, camels, cattle, and sheep, without number, and counted them as spoil." Sennacherib boasts that he has locked Hezekiah in Jerusalem "like a bird in a cage."	In Hezekiah's fourteenth year, "King Sennacherib of Assyria came up against all the fortified cities of Judah and captured them" (18:13). Sennacherib dispatches an army with his general to Jerusalem and effectively blockades the city (18:17–27), being able to boast that the people "are doomed with you to eat their own dung and to drink their own urine" (18:27).
Hezekiah, "overwhelmed by the awesome splendor of my lordship . . . , sent me . . . 30 talents of gold, 800 talents of silver" as well as a long list of precious goods, weapons, "together with his daughters, his palace women," and also a messenger who did obeisance to Sennacherib.	Hezekiah is forced to pay 300 talents of silver, 30 talents of gold, all the silver "in the house of the LORD and in the treasuries of the king's house" as well as the gold "from the doors of the temple" and the doorposts of the palace (18:14b–16).

Possible Conclusions

All of this assumes that the original event recorded or visually depicted actually happened. Given the amount of data available from written, visual, and archaeological remains, there seems little doubt that Sennacherib did in fact invade Judah. If, however, there is any suspicion that these records were fictional or legendary creations intended to provide the king with a positive "spin" on the events, then we are working with an entirely different type of record. Certainly, some of what has been included in the Assyrian annals does stretch the truth and is so exaggerated that it defies the reader's ability to take it at face value. Any account that is produced exclusively for political, theological, or etiological purposes requires the reader to engage in an extensive process of interpretation to determine what is in fact useful information for the reconstruction of history.

Sometimes the process of reconstruction and especially the establishment of a chronology of events is aided by the inclusion of a simple record of natural phenomena such as an earthquake (Amos 1:1) or an eclipse. For instance, the Assyrians, starting in the nineteenth century BCE, created an eponym list that contains the names assigned to each of the years of a reigning king. This list facilitated the dating of commercial transactions, such as leases, and provides modern researchers with a good sequence upon which to base not only a chronology of the Assyrian kings but also of rulers and events in kingdoms mentioned in the Assyrian list (Dever 2001: 160–63). Particularly helpful in this regard is the name of the year 763 BCE, which mentions an eclipse of the sun that can be checked against astronomical records to verify the date. From this solid date it is possible to calculate the date for military campaigns, festivals, coronations, and other major events included in the annals (Millard 1997; Hallo and Younger 1997–2002: 1.466 §136).

Stories that describe supernatural events, such as the origins of the world (creation accounts), or that contain heroic exploits or feats of superhuman strength (such as the Mesopotamian Epic of Gilgamesh) follow a different pattern or composition process—one best examined through literary analysis (see chapter 3). Like the examination of historical records, literary analysis attempts to trace a story back to its origins or social setting and tries to determine what sources it may have used in its composition and the editing process that has shaped it, but it does not start with the premise that it is primarily a record of actual, historical events.

180

Writing a History of Ancient Israel

Having laid out a set of methodological considerations and having developed a basic semiotic pattern of historical interpretation, I would now like to turn to a series of questions that will address whether a history of the ancient Israelites can be written. They will address not only the value of the records and signs that we currently possess but also some of the scholarly positions that have been raised about this process in the past three decades, some of which I have already discussed in chapter 3. In particular I wish to emphasize that the available data is of mixed character. However, used with care and a degree of analytical skepticism, it becomes clear that the ancient Near Eastern texts and the biblical narratives do contain valuable historical information and should not be abandoned or declared too flawed to be used by scholars (Grabbe 2000: 215).

What Do We Really Know about the History of Ancient Israel?

To answer this question, we first need to take stock of our assets. Each of the points below represents either what may have been available to the authors and editors of the biblical text or are the material remains that have been discovered by archaeologists or have become available through the antiquities market:

1. We possess the received biblical text (see chapter 3 for a discussion of textual criticism and existing manuscripts). Modern translations are based on the compilation and analysis of existing manuscripts, none of which are earlier than the second century BCE (Dead Sea Scrolls). Presumably, the biblical authors and editors had at their disposal a store of oral traditions as well as written records to draw upon. However, we do

181

not possess autographs (first editions), and most likely neither did the biblical editors.

2. We have indications within the biblical narrative of the editorial process that the scribes employed in pulling together their interpretation of events. This includes references in the text to a few unfortunately now-lost sources that the authors drew material from as they were composing their writings (Book of Jashar in Josh. 10:13; Book of the Annals of the Kings of Israel in 1 Kings 14:19).

3. Archaeologists have uncovered evidence of the material culture of various periods of occupation in the areas said to have been occupied by the ancient Israelites (see chapter 2). This includes private dwellings, monumental architecture (temples and palaces), and artifacts associated with warfare, religious practices, and economic behavior. All of these artifactual remains serve as a partial and quite fragmentary record of life in ancient Israel. They can help to illuminate some references made in the biblical text to aspects of warfare, farming, marriage customs, religious rituals, economic transactions, and other everyday life activities. However, they cannot tell us the whole story. It requires examination of both the text and the material remains uncovered by archaeologists, bringing the two into dialogue with each other, to advance interpretation toward probability and hypothesis on the reliability of data (Halpern 2000: 119).

4. Extrabiblical monumental inscriptions and administrative documents have been discovered and deciphered from Egypt, Mesopotamia, and Syria-Palestine dating to periods associated with the events described in the biblical narrative (i.e., Merneptah Stele, Mesha Stele, Tel Dan Inscription). These ancient texts have been compiled and translated for scholars and students and serve as a partial repository of the thought and

worldview of these ancient peoples (see the list at the end of this chapter). Although many of them were produced in a different social context than that of ancient Israel, there is evidence of shared cultural elements: law, literature, wisdom. Again, however, they provide only a fragmentary and in some cases nonrepresentative cross section of the literature and economic and political documents produced in antiquity. While they are important, simply because they are among the few that have been recovered does not make them automatically the key to understanding ancient Israel (Barstad 1997: 50).

From this data we can formulate a plausible hypothesis that ancient Israel existed and that it functioned as a recognizable political entity during a set period of time, say between 1000 BCE and 400 BCE. As it currently stands, the data cannot prove the existence of the kings of the early monarchy (Saul, David, and Solomon), but a lack of data should not be considered convincing since the records from Mesopotamia that mention the kings of Israel starting in the ninth century BCE provide the plausibility that earlier kings did exist (Grabbe 2000: 216). The corroboration of accounts in the biblical narrative and ancient Near Eastern records (e.g., the siege of Jerusalem in 701 BCE by King Sennacherib of Assyria) also helps us create a tentative chronology of events. Examination of architectural remains, destruction layers, and inscriptional materials (i.e., Lachish Letters or the *lmlk* seal impressions) provides sufficient physical evidence to make a case for a level of social organization, political sophistication, and economic development associated with small nation-states. However, it is still necessary to be cautious about the exact details of the development of these social changes until additional data are discovered or culled from existing texts.

Can the Biblical Account Be Utilized as a Source for Writing a History of Israel?

In recent years, the historical value of the biblical narrative has been questioned by some scholars, who have chosen to dismiss the biblical account as a fabrication of the postexilic or even the Hellenistic period (Thompson 1992; Lemche 1988; 2001; Whitelam 1996). However, their hypercritical, minimalist attitude can block interpretative paths by dismissing a whole body of data (Laato 2005). Admittedly, the editing process that contributed to the systematic compilation of much of the biblical record did take place in the period after 600 BCE. That does not, however, negate the likelihood that portions of this record predate that period and in fact represent earlier traditions and accounts. Simply because the Deuteronomistic Historian or the Chronicler chose to shape Israel's narrative history in a certain manner, including certain details, literary genres, and subplots (e.g., the "sin" of Jeroboam in 1 Kings 12:25–33 as the basis for national degradation), does not mean that this is all fictional material or that it did "not spring from earlier traditions" (Barstad 1997: 57–58).

History and historicity are not always the same thing. The story that a people tells about itself is not its whole history—it is the filtered narrative that they tell about themselves. To make this even clearer, let us use the definition of narrative provided by L. G. Stone: narrative "is the organization of material in a chronologically sequential order" that focuses the content on a "single coherent story," including subplots (1979: 3). While a narrative may contain some historical data (personages, places, events), it is not an attempt to create an objective analysis. In other words, people tell the story about themselves that they want to hear. Furthermore, it does not remain static and unchanged as long as it is transmitted orally; it continually evolves, with new details being added and irrelevant or no longer understood elements being removed.

A. Graeme Auld, for instance, suggests that "the interrelationships of Samuel–Kings and Chronicles" can be explained through the process of "independent supplementation of a common inherited text" (1994: 4). Furthermore, even when a narrative is given the status of canonical literature, it will continue to be interpreted to fit the agenda and cultural understanding of later affectants.

To illustrate this process, let us briefly examine the character of two of the main interpretative voices evident in the biblical narrative: the Deuteronomistic Historian and the Chronicler. While there are many different interpretations of these revisionist histories of ancient Israel, I will try to highlight current scholarly trends. For example, nearly all scholars suggest that the Deuteronomistic Historian drew upon earlier traditions for the creation of much of the current narrative. However, there is disagreement about when the editing process took place and how many subsequent sets of editors had an influence on the shaping of the narrative (Campbell and O'Brien 2000: 11–17). As the narrative in Deuteronomy through 2 Kings unfolds, there seems to be an alternation between two views of history. One is a positive view of the nation's future indicating that all of God's covenantal promises will be fulfilled and that the monarchy, once it has been established, will successfully guide the people (Deut. 30:11–14; Josh. 21:45; 2 Sam. 7:16). This alternates with periodic warnings in the narrative about the consequences of disobedience to the law or the covenant with God (Josh. 1:7–9; 1 Sam. 8:7–8; 2 Kings 17:7–20). In particular, there are negative and judgmental evaluations injected into the recitation of the acts of particular kings (Solomon's apostasy in 1 Kings 11:1–13; Jeroboam's sin in 1 Kings 12:25–33; Manasseh's unfaithfulness to the covenant in 2 Kings 21:1–9). These are suggestive of the revision process and the reinterpretation of the events of past history. They allow the affectant editors, working in part with earlier traditions, to take a more critical view and provide them with the justification for their determination that events in their own time can be explained through this reading of prior history.

Since by its nature the process of editing includes an attempt to reshape the material, it should not be surprising to find that it sometimes attempts to achieve an idealized or whitewashed version, deleting or minimizing negative facts or impressions. This seems to be the case in the work of the biblical editor known as the Chronicler, writing in the late fourth century BCE. This team of editors/affectants employed the earlier Deuteronomistic History and other sources in their compilation of events but chose to leave some events out of their narrative, as might be expected of a trained team of historiographers "writing in accord with the accepted practices" of their own time (Japhet 1993: 25–28; Hoglund 1997: 28–29).

One of the examples of this shaping process can be found in a comparison with the Deuteronomistic Historian's portrayal of the events that led up to the secession of the northern tribes. This earlier recitation of events points directly to Solomon's apostasies (building shrines for his foreign wives' gods) as a prime cause of the fracturing of the nation. It also indicates that the political crisis was in part the result of Rehoboam's diplomatic failure to successfully negotiate with the unhappy tribal elders at Shechem (1 Kings 11:1–12:19). This in turn led to Ahijah's prophetic oracle (11:29–39) that granted Jeroboam the right to rule over the northern tribes (Knoppers 1990: 428).

In contrast, the Chronicler did not wish to place any blame on Solomon or on any Davidic king. Instead, this affectant's explanation for the division of the kingdom is related in a "call to return" speech by Abijah, Rehoboam's son (2 Chron. 13:4–12) (Throntveit 1997: 230). In this contrived piece of political rhetoric, Abijah accuses Jeroboam and the "worthless scoundrels" who had rallied to his rebellious call of taking advantage of a young, inexperienced ruler, who "could not withstand them" (13:6–7). Furthermore, the argument is made that Jeroboam's actions and the secession of the northern tribes were totally illegal because they ignored the political rights of the House of David, which had been granted to them by Yahweh as an everlasting "covenant of salt" (13:5). Abijah then asserts in his "battlefield speech" that the northern tribes' hopes for military victory or their hopes of remaining a part of the covenantal community are forlorn as long as they reject God's covenant and obey Jeroboam's idolatrous orders (13:8–12). They must now recognize their errors and accept Davidic rule and the supremacy of Jerusalem (Knoppers 1990: 437, 440). In that way, they can rejoin the company of "brothers" that comprise the people of God (Throntveit 1997: 243).

How Do We Create a Dialogue between Biblical Narrative, Extrabiblical Texts, and Archaeological Data?

Based upon the methodological framework that I have developed throughout this volume, I would like to take a critical look at a portion of the biblical narrative (1 Kings 16) that deals with the rather chaotic and unstable era immediately following the division of the kingdom. The Deuteronomistic Historian has shaped the narrative in such a way that Israel's instability is highlighted and its kings demonized for their willingness to continue to "walk in the way of Jeroboam." However, the narrative also mentions the construction of a new capital city for Israel at Samaria and includes events in the reigns of two kings who are well known outside the Bible.

To make this reading more coherent, I will lay out a few background points from the biblical narrative as it is shaped by the Deuteronomistic Historian. What appears here is a cyclic framework that is reminiscent of the cycle that serves as a literary foundation for the period of the judges (Matthews 2004b: 8; Halpern 1988: 151–52).

187

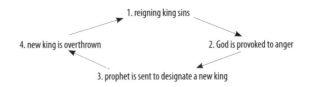

1. **Reigning king sins** Because of Solomon's apostasy, Rehoboam's failed diplomacy, and the designation of the prophet Ahijah, Jeroboam is proclaimed king of the northern kingdom. He then initiates a series of steps designed to create a separate national identity for Israel and to wean the people away from the Davidic kingship and from Jerusalem as the central cultic site. The Deuteronomistic Historian calls this "Jeroboam's sin" (1 Kings 12:25–33) and uses it as the foundation for his argument that the kings of Israel have rejected the covenant with Yahweh and therefore deserve the periodic rebellions staged by their leaders and ultimately the destruction of the northern kingdom by the Assyrians.

2. **God is provoked to anger** The immediate response to Jeroboam's actions is the condemnation of his royal house by the prophet Ahijah (1 Kings 14:7–16). The prophet's message takes the form of a curse on all of Jeroboam's family and lays them open to being overthrown. This stands in stark contrast to the "everlasting covenant" that God (as proclaimed by the prophet Nathan) made with David's house in Judah and Jerusalem (2 Sam. 7:4–16; 1 Kings 9:1–5).

3. **Prophet is sent to designate a new king** Fulfilling Ahijah's prophecy, Jeroboam's son Nadab reigns only two years before he is overthrown by Baasha, whom the prophet Jehu proclaims God had "exalted . . . out of the dust" to become Israel's leader (1 Kings 16:2). The entire family of Jeroboam is killed. The editor indicates that this misfortune is based on Jeroboam's sins, which

he "caused Israel to commit, and because of the anger to which he provoked the LORD" (15:27–30).

4. **New king is overthrown**   After reigning twenty-four years, Baasha is also overthrown by a rebellious military commander, Zimri, and the editor's explanation is that Baasha had "walked in the way of Jeroboam" (16:1–2, 5–7).

With this material as background, we now see how in the aftermath of Baasha's rebellion against Nadab the cycle continues to function in subsequent reigns. In taking the throne by force and eliminating the family of the reigning monarch, Baasha had set a precedent that would eventually come back to haunt him. It is not surprising then that this formulaic narrative in 1 Kings 16 begins with a condemning statement by yet another prophet, Jehu ben Hanani (Cogan 2001: 410, 412). Baasha is told that God has again been provoked to anger by a king, who had been "exalted . . . out of the dust" (i.e., raised to leadership even though he, like Jeroboam, was not a member of the royal house) and yet has "walked in the way of Jeroboam" (1 Kings 16:1–2). Because of God's anger, Baasha's house will be "utterly swept away." In essence they will be returned to the dust (i.e., to nonroyal status) from which they had come (Brueggemann 1972: 2; compare similar language in Gen. 3:19).

In a narrative repetition of the story of the destruction of Jeroboam's house, Baasha's son Elah is killed after reigning just two years, and is replaced by one of his chariot commanders, Zimri (1 Kings 16:8–10). This upstart, however, rules for only seven days, and his only accomplishment is the murder of all the members of Baasha's house, again with the editorial note that this was a fulfillment of the curse against Baasha for his idolatrous acts (16:11–13). Zimri's usurpation of the throne apparently did not have the support of the rest of the troops, and when he saw that he could not hold the capital city of Tirzah, he committed suicide, leaving the throne to yet

189

another army commander, Omri (16:15–18). And, in order to comply with the strict literary and theological structure of this account, even Zimri is said, during his brief reign, to have committed the sins of Jeroboam (16:19).

To this point there has been a rapid succession of kings, none of whom has been able to pass on his kingdom and authority for any length of time (two years seems to be the standard measure) to his son. Omri, once he overcomes a challenge from another claimant to the throne (Tibni ben Ginath in 1 Kings 16:21–22), breaks this mold at last and brings relative stability to the nation by establishing a dynasty that will last three generations. He is also said to have moved the capital city to the "hill of Samaria," where he constructed a new fortress as his seat of government (16:24). That, however, is all that the biblical editor is willing to say about this monarch except for the usual epithet that he did "evil in the sight of the LORD . . . provoking the LORD . . . to anger by their idols" (16:25–26). The editors even deny him a patronym (a reference to his father), and this may actually be evidence that Omri was not an Israelite but a foreign usurper, possibly even a Phoenician, since his son, Ahab, later marries a Phoenician princess (Kuan 1993: 232–33).

First Kings 16 then concludes with the succession of Ahab as king of Israel and his marriage, like Solomon, to a foreign wife, Jezebel, the daughter of the king of Sidon in Phoenicia (16:29–33). Since this Omride dynasty does in fact last for a while, the editor must abandon the previous narrative formula, and so he injects into Ahab's royal chronicle the statement that he "did evil in the sight of the LORD more than all who were before him" (16:30). To enlarge on this judgment, the editor then cites several specifics in a manner that could be compared to a legal brief (16:31–33). Once this narrative detour has been completed, the reader is directed back to the original cycle (Wallace 1986: 30–32). The sinful king Ahab and his house are cursed by the prophet Elijah (21:17–26); Jehu ben Jehoshaphat is designated as the divinely chosen usurper to Israel's throne by the prophet Elisha (2 Kings 9); and the entire House of Ahab (i.e., all those with kinship ties either by blood or association) is massacred (10:1–11).

Archaeology and Extrabiblical Texts in Dialogue with 1 Kings 16

Of the kings listed in 1 Kings 16, only Omri and Ahab are mentioned in extrabiblical texts. The rather sparse references to these two Omride kings in the biblical narrative make it necessary to turn to the physical remains of the capital at Samaria and to extrabiblical documents to build on what we can learn about this period of Israel's history.

1. Omri is said to have purchased the estate of Shemer as the site for his new capital. He then named the city Samaria, thereby attaching it to the ancestral name of the family from the tribe of Issachar that originally had settled there (1 Kings 16:23–24) (B. Mazar 1989). A survey of the site and a series of excavations have demonstrated that a large estate originally occupied the hilltop. Ceramic remains indicate that "there must have been continual activity on the hill from at least the 11th century B.C. until it was bought by Omri in the early ninth century B.C." (Stager 1990: 103). This interpretation is enhanced by the discovery of numerous bottle-shaped cisterns and associated olive oil- and wine-processing installations carved into the bedrock (Franklin 2004: 192). There is also evidence of extensive hillside terracing, which would have accommodated the cultivation of olive trees and vineyards that produced the cash crops on the estate. These facilities would have contributed to the lucrative oil and wine industry in the southern region of Samaria upon which much of Israel's economy was based

(Finkelstein 1999: 42). In fact, the large capacity of oil and wine produced by Shemer's estate on this hilltop site may have helped to lure Omri into purchasing it as a means of financing the construction of his palace (Franklin 2004: 194, 201). This could explain why only a portion of the summit of the hill was scraped away to bedrock and shaped to form a platform for monumental buildings (Ussishkin 1997b: 358). Not surprisingly, the olive and winepresses were left intact to continue to produce a steady income for the king and his government. Since Omri ruled only seven years, the majority of the monumental remains, including a royal palace, are most likely attributable to his son and successor Ahab (Dever 2001: 164). The initial building period therefore set the stage for greater efforts by Omri's successors. Furthermore, the cisterns and rock-cut presses remained in use until Building Period II, when the entire summit of Samaria was transformed into an administrative center by Jehu and the later kings of Israel (Franklin 2004: 200–201).

2. The relative importance of Omri as the founder of a dynasty of kings in Israel is further authenticated by a reference to *bīt-ḫumrî* ("House of Omri") in the Assyrian royal annals of Shalmaneser III, inscribed on two monumental bulls found at Calah, dating to about 841 BCE (Hallo and Younger 1997–2002: 2.267 §113C). This serves as the Assyrian designation for the kingdom of Israel, named for the founder of its ruling house (Na'aman 1998: 236). It seems a bit ironic that the reference is actually associated with Jehu, who was responsible, according to the biblical account (2 Kings 10:1–17), for eliminating all representatives of the House of Ahab and thereby bringing the Omride dynasty to an end. The question then is why Jehu would be referred to by the Assyrians as *mār-ḫumrî* ("son of Omri"). Our answer may be found

in the specific political attitude the Assyrians were expressing by using this designation. Indications are that almost immediately after seizing the throne Jehu submitted to the Assyrian king and paid tribute, an act graphically portrayed in the Black Obelisk Inscription of Shalmaneser III (Hallo and Younger 1997–2002: 2.270 §113F). Because of this the Assyrians apparently were willing to legitimize his position as king of Israel. Being named "son of Omri" therefore functions as a reward for a faithful and loyal vassal, who has eliminated an enemy ruler. It also functions as a signal, couched in propagandistic terms, to other would-be usurpers who might be of service to the Assyrians in the future (Na'aman 1998: 237).

Shalmaneser III's Black Obelisk Inscription (Jehu's obeisance)

3. Omri's establishment of economic alliances and vassalage arrangements with neighboring states would have helped them to create a united front against their enemies. It can be surmised that these smaller states were attempting to strengthen themselves in the face of increasing pressure from the Assyrian Empire. One direct result of this process was the formation of an anti-Assyrian Damascus-led coalition, which according to the Assyrian annals included a large contingent of chariots led by King Ahab (Hallo and Younger 1997–2002: 2.263 §113A). Standing together, they temporar-

ily were able to withstand the Assyrians at the battle of Qarqar in 853 BCE, although King Shalmaneser III of Assyria still claimed to have achieved a great victory (Tadmor 1975: 38–40; Dearman 1989: 158–59). Falling into the pattern or the tendency in Assyrian records to claim much while admitting—through the inclusion of subsequent struggles and imposition of tribute—that victories are not always complete, Shalmaneser had to cope with this coalition for the next decade as he continued to campaign in Syria-Palestine (Grayson 2004–5). True to the anti-Omride theme of the Deuteronomistic Historian, the biblical narrative does not mention Ahab's involvement in the Damascus coalition and tends to emphasize his weakness of character. The biblical narrative does contain a mixed relationship between Israel and Aram (Syria), with periods of both peace and war (1 Kings 20:1–34; 22:1–36). However, this does not preclude the possibility that Ahab was allied with Damascus during the Qarqar campaign; it simply demonstrates that the biblical editor chose not to mention it in his royal annals and instead chose to focus on negative events and judgments (Long 2002: 371–72).

4. Omri's name also appears in the inscription created to celebrate the declared victory of King Mesha of Moab over a "son of Omri." A somewhat different account of these events is recorded in 2 Kings 3. The Moabite Inscription or Mesha Stele commemorating King Mesha's liberation of his country from Israelite control dates to approximately 840 BCE. It is an artful piece of political rhetoric written to justify Mesha's invasion of the land of Madaba, north of Moab's traditional border at the Wadi el-Mujib (River Arnon). The text chronicles the Moabite king's success in liberating his people from a forty-year period of foreign control by the Israelites, which had begun in his father's reign. It does not specifi-

cally mention Ahab, and the revolt itself probably took place in Joram's reign, a better fit with the forty-year chronology described in the text (Long 2002: 374).

The primary reason given in the Mesha Stele for Israel's domination of Moab is the anger of their national god, Chemosh, a theme well developed in the book of Judges (Judg. 3:12–14). This admission may in fact represent evidence of the ability of Omri and his successors to extend their hegemony into Transjordan during the ninth century. Omri had already established an alliance with the Phoenicians through the marriage of his son Ahab to Jezebel (1 Kings 16:31). This gave him an economic link to seagoing trade in the Mediterranean Sea. He may, therefore, have wished to expand his economic enterprises eastward into the Moabite Plateau north of the Arnon River by gaining some control over the King's Highway, which linked Damascus to the Gulf of Aqaba in the south (Na'aman 1997: 90–91).

While Omri and Ahab were able to hold together political and economic agreements among the allied states, Ahab's son Joram/Jehoram could not withstand the rapacious efforts of the Aramean king Hazael (2 Kings 9:15), and as a result Israel lost its effective control over northern and central Transjordan. Sensing this growing weakness, Mesha's break from Israelite control would have begun with his refusal to pay tribute and his subsequent military preparations following Ahab's death (Smelik 1990). When he saw that Ahab's successors made no moves to prevent the consolidation of his rule over the northern Moabite plateau, Mesha would have felt safe in taking over the Gadite cities of Ataroth and Nebo and the Israelite outpost at Jahaz (Miller 1989: 39). In the process, he certainly would have reclaimed control over the King's Highway, facilitating the reconstruction of his country's cities and his economy; line 26 of the Moabite Inscription reads: "I built Aroer and made the highway at the Arnon" (Jackson 1989: 98).

Concluding Remarks

What our examination of this biblical narrative in dialogue with extrabiblical texts and archaeological remains suggests is that our picture and our understanding of the events described in these texts is incomplete. That is exactly the point that needs to be made—not that our sources are without merit, entirely fictional, or intentionally misleading. The potential interpretants available to us from existing data allow for a variety of interpretative paths, some more credible than others. It is the task of the historian of ancient Israel to gather all available information—including the biblical text (Miller 1991b)—piece it together in a variety of ways, and posit an interpretation based on clearly defined research methodologies that do justice to the data while keeping in mind the potential for shaping of the material both in antiquity and today. Each chapter in this volume has pointed the way to gathering that data and employing a variety of methods to interpret it. As critical readers of ancient texts, examiners of scientific data such as climatological records or spectroscopic

---

Exercises in History Writing

Consider for a moment the task of producing a historical narrative of an event that occurred in ancient Israel. If you are an ancient scribe living during the reign of King Josiah in Judah (640–609 BCE), how would you begin your task? What sources would you draw on? Who would you talk to about what you are reading? How will you decide what to select from your sources for inclusion in your account? What political or religious influences would guide your interpretation of your sources? Would you even give a thought to producing an objective version of events?

On the other hand, if you are a modern scholar who wishes to write a historical account of a specific event during the time period of ancient Israel, how does your task differ from that of the scribe in Josiah's day? Will you be able to draw on the same set of data available to the ancient scribe? To what degree will you rely on archaeological and ethnographic findings? How will you determine the referential world of the writers of your sources? How will you be influenced in your interpretation by your own political and social views?

analysis of ceramics, social scientists, or historians, we will ultimately make judgments that will become signs. These signs, in and of themselves, are a satisfying, even enjoyable, product of personal research, but they will also serve, once they are published, as referents from which later generations will draw meaning and thus continue the endless cycle.

Histories of Ancient Israel

Ahlstrom, Gösta W. 1993. *The History of Ancient Palestine from the Paleolithic Period to Alexander's Conquest*. Sheffield: Sheffield Academic Press.

Lemche, Niels P. 1988. *Ancient Israel: A New History of Israelite Society*. Sheffield: JSOT Press.

Matthews, Victor H. 2002. *A Brief History of Ancient Israel*. Louisville: Westminster/John Knox.

Miller, J. Maxwell, and John H. Hayes. 2006. *A History of Ancient Israel and Judah*. 2nd ed. Louisville: Westminster/John Knox.

Provan, Iain W., V. Phillips Long, and Tremper Longman III. 2003. *A Biblical History of Israel*. Louisville: Westminster/John Knox.

Soggin, J. Alberto. 1984. *A History of Ancient Israel*. Translated by John Bowden. Philadelphia: Westminster.

Ancient Near Eastern Texts in Translation

Beyerlin, Walter, ed. 1978. *Near Eastern Religious Texts Relating to the Old Testament*. Translated by John Bowden. Philadelphia: Westminster.

Hallo, William W., and K. Lawson Younger Jr., eds. 1997–2002. *The Context of Scripture*. 3 vols. Leiden: Brill.

Matthews, Victor H., and Don C. Benjamin. 2006. *Old Testament Parallels: Laws and Stories from the Ancient Near East*. 3rd ed. Mahwah, NJ: Paulist.

Pritchard, James, ed. 1969. *Ancient Near Eastern Texts Relating to the Old Testament*. 3rd ed. Princeton: Princeton University Press.

References

Aharoni, Yohanan. 1979. *The Land of the Bible: A Historical Geography*. Philadelphia: Westminster.

Aharoni, Yohanan, Michael Avi-Yonah, Anson F. Rainey, and Ze'ev Safrai. 1993. *The Macmillan Bible Atlas*. 3rd ed. New York: Macmillan.

Ahlstrom, Gösta W. 1993. *The History of Ancient Palestine from the Paleolithic Period to Alexander's Conquest*. Sheffield: Sheffield Academic Press.

Allen, John. 1999. "Spacial Assemblages of Power: From Domination to Empowerment." In *Human Geography Today*, edited by Doreen Massey, John Allen, and Philip Sarre, 194–218. Cambridge: Polity Press.

Alter, Robert. 1981. *The Art of Biblical Narrative*. New York: Basic Books.

Artzy, Michal. 1998. "Routes, Trade, Boats, and 'Nomads of the Sea.'" In *Mediterranean Peoples in Transition, Thirteenth to Early Tenth Centuries BCE*, edited by Seymour Gitin et al., 439–48. Jerusalem: Israel Exploration Society.

Astour, Michael. 1995. "Overland Trade Routes in Ancient Western Asia." In *Civilizations of the Ancient Near East*, edited by Jack M. Sasson, 1401–20. New York: Scribner.

Auld, A. Graeme. 1978. "Cities of Refuge in Israelite Tradition." *Journal for the Study of the Old Testament* 10:26–40.

———. 1994. *Kings without Privilege: David and Moses in the Story of the Bible's Kings*. Edinburgh: Clark.

199

————. 2000. "The Deuteronomists between History and Theology." In *Congress Volume: Oslo 1998*, edited by André Lemaire and Magne Saebø, 353–67. Vetus Testamentum Supplement 80. Leiden: Brill.

Avigad, Nahman. 1980. "The Chief of the Corvée." *Israel Exploration Journal* 30:170–73.

Barstad, Hans M. 1997. "History and the Hebrew Bible." In *Can a "History of Israel" Be Written?*, edited by Lester L. Grabbe, 37–64. Journal for the Study of the Old Testament Supplement 245. Sheffield: Sheffield Academic Press.

Barthes, Roland. 1977. "Rhetoric of the Image." In Barthes's *Image, Music, Text*, 32–51. Translated by Stephen Heath. New York: Hill & Wang.

Barton, John. 2003. "Canonical Approaches Ancient and Modern." In *Biblical Canons*, edited by J.-M. Auwers and H. J. de Jonge, 199–209. Leuven: Leuven University Press.

Becking, Bob. 2003. "Chronology: A Skeleton without Flesh? Sennacherib's Campaign as a Case-Study." In *"Like a Bird in a Cage": The Invasion of Sennacherib in 701 BCE*, edited by Lester L. Grabbe, 46–72. Journal for the Study of the Old Testament Supplement 363. New York: Sheffield Academic Press.

Beek, Martinus A. 1994. "David and Absalom: A Hebrew Tragedy in Prose." In *Voices from Amsterdam: A Modern Tradition of Reading Biblical Narrative*, edited by Martin Kessler, 155–68. Atlanta: Scholars Press.

Beitzel, Barry J. 1985. *The Moody Atlas of Bible Lands*. Chicago: Moody.

Ben-Tor, Amnon, ed. 1994. *The Archaeology of Ancient Israel*. New Haven: Yale University Press.

Berquist, Jon L. 2002. "Critical Spatiality and the Construction of the Ancient World." In *"Imagining" Biblical Worlds: Studies in Spatial, Social, and Historical Constructs in Honor of James W. Flanagan*, edited by David M. Gunn and Paula M. McNutt, 14–29. Journal for the Study of the Old Testament Supplement 359. New York: Sheffield Academic Press.

Beyerlin, Walter, ed. 1978. *Near Eastern Religious Texts Relating to the Old Testament*. Translated by John Bowden. Philadelphia: Westminster.

Bimson, John J., and J. P. Kane. 1985. *The New Bible Atlas*. Leicester: Inter-Varsity.

Black, Jeremy. 1997. *Maps and History: Constructing Images of the Past*. New Haven: Yale University Press.

Bloch-Smith, Elizabeth. 2002. "Life in Judah from the Perspective of the Dead." *Near Eastern Archaeology* 65:120–30.

————. 2004. "Resurrecting the Iron I Dead." *Israel Exploration Journal* 54:77–91.

Bloch-Smith, Elizabeth, and Beth Nakai. 1999. "A Landscape Comes to Life: The Iron Age I." *Near Eastern Archaeology* 62:62–92.

Boadt, Lawrence. 1983. "Intentional Alliteration in Second Isaiah." *Catholic Biblical Quarterly* 45:353–63.

Borowski, Oded. 1987. *Agriculture in Iron Age Israel.* Winona Lake, IN: Eisenbrauns.

Bourdieu, Pierre. 1989. "Social Space and Symbolic Power." *Sociological Theory* 7:14–25.

Bradley, Richard. 1997. "'To See Is to Have Seen': Craft Traditions in British Field Archaeology." In *The Cultural Life of Images: Visual Representation in Archaeology*, edited by Brian L. Molyneaux, 62–72. London: Routledge.

Braybrooke, Marcus, and James Harpur, eds. 1999. *Collegeville Bible Atlas.* Collegeville, MN: Liturgical Press.

Briggs, Richard S. 2002. "The Implied Author and the Creation of the World: A Test Case in Reader-Response Criticism." *Expository Times* 113:264–70.

Brisco, Thomas C. 1999. *Holman Bible Atlas: A Complete Guide to the Expansive Geography of Biblical History.* Nashville: Broadman & Holman.

Brueggemann, Walter. 1972. "From Dust to Kingship." *Zeitschrift für die alttestamentliche Wissenschaft* 84:1–18.

Buchler, Justus, ed. 1955. *Philosophical Writings of Pierce.* New York: Dover.

Cahill, Jane M. 2003. "Jerusalem at the Time of the United Monarchy: The Archaeological Evidence." In *Jerusalem in Bible and Archaeology: The First Temple Period*, edited by Andrew G. Vaughn and Ann E. Killebrew, 13–80. Atlanta: Society of Biblical Literature.

————. 2004. "Jerusalem in David and Solomon's Time: It Really Was a Major City in the Tenth Century B.C.E." *Biblical Archaeology Review* 30.6:20–31, 62–63.

Campbell, Antony F., and Mark A. O'Brien. 2000. *Unfolding the Deuteronomistic History.* Minneapolis: Fortress.

Carter, Charles E. 1996. "A Discipline in Transition: The Contributions of the Social Sciences to the Study of the Hebrew Bible." In *Community, Identity, and Ideology: Social Science Approaches to the Hebrew Bible*, edited by Charles E. Carter and Carol L. Meyers, 3–36. Winona Lake, IN: Eisenbrauns.

Casson, Lionel. 1974. *Travel in the Ancient World*. London: Allen.

Chalcraft, David J., ed. 1997. *Social Scientific Old Testament Criticism*. Biblical Seminar 47. Sheffield: Sheffield Academic Press.

Chaney, Marvin. 1983. "Ancient Palestinian Peasant Movements and the Formation of Pre-monarchic Israel." In *Palestine in Transition: The Emergence of Ancient Israel*, edited by D. N. Freedman and D. F. Graf, 39–90. Sheffield: Almond.

Childs, Brevard S. 1979. *Introduction to the Old Testament as Scripture*. Philadelphia: Fortress.

Chilton, Bruce D. 1997. "Biblical Authority, Canonical Criticism, and Generative Exegesis." In *Quest for Context and Meaning*, edited by Craig Evans and Shemaryahu Talmon, 343–55. Leiden: Brill.

Chisholm, Robert. 1990. "'For Three Sins . . . Even for Four': The Numerical Sayings in Amos." *Bibliotheca sacra* 147:188–97.

Clancy, Frank. 1999. "Shishak/Shoshenq's Travels." *Journal for the Study of the Old Testament* 86:3–23.

Clark, Douglas R. 2003. "Bricks, Sweat, and Tears: The Human Investment in Constructing a 'Four-Room' House." *Near Eastern Archaeology* 66:34–43.

Cogan, Mordechai. 2001. *1 Kings*. Anchor Bible 10. New York: Doubleday.

Cohn, Robert L. 1982. "The Literary Logic of 1 Kings 17–19." *Journal of Biblical Literature* 101:333–50.

Coleman, John A. 1999. "The Bible and Sociology." *Sociology of Religion* 60:125–48.

Collins, Randall. 1994. *Four Sociological Traditions*. New York: Oxford University Press.

Cresswell, Tim. 1996. *In Place, Out of Place: Geography, Ideology, and Transgression*. Minneapolis: University of Minnesota Press.

Crook, Zeba A. 2006. "Reciprocity: Covenantal Exchange as a Test Case." In *Ancient Israel: The Old Testament in Its Social Context*, edited by Philip F. Esler, 78–91. Minneapolis: Fortress.

Dalley, Stephanie. 1984. *Mari and Karana: Two Old Babylonian Cities*. London: Longman.

Darby, H. C. 1962. "Historical Geography." In *Approaches to History*, edited by H. P. R. Finberg, 127–56. Toronto: University of Toronto Press.

Daube, David. 1998. "Absalom and the Ideal King." *Vetus Testamentum* 48:315–25.

David, Nicholas, and Carol Kramer. 2001. *Ethnoarchaeology in Action*. New York: Cambridge University Press.

Davies, Philip R. 2000. "What Separates a Minimalist from a Maximalist? Not Much." *Biblical Archaeology Review* 26.2:24–27, 72–73.

Davis, Thomas W. 2004. "Theory and Method in Biblical Archaeology." In *The Future of Biblical Archaeology: Reassessing Methodologies and Assumptions*, edited by James K. Hoffmeier and Alan R. Millard, 20–28. Grand Rapids: Eerdmans.

Dearman, J. Andrew. 1989. "Historical Reconstruction and the Mesha Inscription." In *Studies in the Mesha Inscription and Moab*, edited by J. Andrew Dearman, 155–210. Atlanta: Scholars Press.

Dever, William G. 1997. "On Listening to the Text—and the Artifacts." In *The Echoes of Many Texts: Reflections on Jewish and Christian Traditions*, edited by William G. Dever and J. Edward Wright, 1–23. Atlanta: Scholars Press.

———. 1998. "Israelite Origins and the 'Nomadic Ideal': Can Archaeology Separate Fact from Ficton?" In *Mediterranean Peoples in Transition: Thirteenth to Early Tenth Centuries BCE*, edited by Seymour Gitin, Amihai Mazar, and Ephraim Stern, 220–37. Jerusalem: Israel Exploration Society.

———. 2001. *What Did the Biblical Writers Know and When Did They Know It? What Archaeology Can Tell Us about the Reality of Ancient Israel*. Grand Rapids: Eerdmans.

———. 2004. "Histories and Non-Histories of Ancient Israel: The Question of the United Monarchy." In *In Search of Pre-exilic Israel*, edited by John Day, 65–94. New York: Clark.

Donaldson, M. E. 1981. "Kinship Theory in the Patriarchal Narratives: The Case of the Barren Wife." *Journal for the American Academy of Religion* 49:77–87.

Dorsey, David A. 1991. *The Roads and Highways of Ancient Israel*. Baltimore: Johns Hopkins University Press.

Douglas, Mary. 1966. *Purity and Danger: An Analysis of Concepts of Pollution and Taboo*. London: Routledge & Kegan Paul.

Durkheim, Émile. 1954. *The Elementary Forms of Religious Life*. Translated by Karen E. Fields. Reprinted New York: Free Press (orig. 1915).

———. 1972. *Selected Writings*. Edited by A. Giddens. Cambridge: Cambridge University Press.

Edelman, Diana V. 1991. *The Fabric of History: Text, Artifact, and Israel's Past*. Sheffield: Sheffield Academic Press.

———. 2000. "What If We Had No Accounts of Sennacherib's Third Campaign or the Palace Reliefs Depicting His Capture of Lachish?"

In *Virtual History and the Bible*, edited by J. Cheryl Exum, 88–103. Leiden: Brill.

Eilberg-Schwartz, Howard. 1990. *The Savage in Judaism: An Anthropology of Israelite Religion and Ancient Judaism*. Bloomington: Indiana University Press.

Eliade, Mircea. 1959. *The Sacred and the Profane: The Nature of Religion*. New York: Harcourt, Brace & World.

Esler, Philip F., and Anselm C. Hagedorn. 2006. "Social-Scientific Analysis of the Old Testament: A Brief History and Overview." In *Ancient Israel: The Old Testament in Its Social Context*, edited by Philip F. Esler, 15–32. Minneapolis: Fortress.

Faust, Avraham. 2005. "The Israelite Village: Cultural Conservatism and Technological Innovation." *Tel Aviv* 32:204–19.

Faust, Avraham, and S. Bunimovitz. 2003. "The Four-Room House: Embodying Iron Age Israelite Society." *Near Eastern Archaeology* 66:22–31.

Faust, Avraham, and Ze'ev Safrai. 2005. "Salvage Excavations as a Source for Reconstructing Settlement History in Ancient Israel." *Palestine Exploration Quarterly* 137:139–58.

Fiensy, David. 1987. "Using the Nuer Culture of Africa in Understanding the Old Testament: An Evaluation." *Journal for the Study of the Old Testament* 38:73–83.

Finkelstein, Israel. 1988. *The Archaeology of the Israelite Settlement*. Jerusalem: Israel Exploration Society.

———. 1989. "The Emergence of the Monarchy in Israel: The Environmental and Socio-Economic Aspects." *Journal for the Study of the Old Testament* 44:43–74.

———. 1995. *Living on the Fringe: The Archaeology and History of the Negev, Sinai, and Neighbouring Regions in the Bronze and Iron Ages*. Sheffield: Sheffield Academic Press.

———. 1999. "State Formation in Israel and Judah: A Contrast in Contexts, a Contrast in Trajectory." *Near Eastern Archaeology* 62:35–52.

———. 2003. "The Rise of Jerusalem and Judah: The Missing Link." In *Jerusalem in Bible and Archaeology*, edited by Andrew G. Vaughn and Ann E. Killigrew, 81–101. Atlanta: Society of Biblical Literature.

Finkelstein, Israel, and Neil A. Silberman. 2001. *The Bible Unearthed: Archaeology's New Vision of Ancient Israel and the Origin of Its Sacred Texts*. New York: Free Press.

———. 2006. *David and Solomon: In Search of the Bible's Sacred Kings and the Roots of the Western Tradition*. New York: Free Press.

Finley, Moses I. 1975. *The Use and Abuse of History*. New York: Viking.

Flanagan, James W. 1988. *David's Social Drama*. Sheffield: Almond.

———. 1999. "Ancient Perceptions of Space/Perceptions of Ancient Space." *Semeia* 87:15–43.

Franklin, Norma. 2004. "Samaria: From the Bedrock to the Omride Palace." *Levant* 36:189–202.

Frick, Frank S. 1985. *The Formation of the State in Ancient Israel*. Sheffield: Almond.

Frolov, Serge. 2002. "Succession Narrative: A 'Document' or a Phantom?" *Journal of Biblical Literature* 121:81–104.

Frolov, Serge, and Vladimir Orel. 1999. "David in Jerusalem." *Zeitschrift für die alttestamentliche Wissenschaft* 111:609–15.

Gallagher, William R. 1999. *Sennacherib's Campaign to Judah: New Studies*. Leiden: Brill.

Geller, Markham J. 1995. "The Influence of Ancient Mesopotamia on Hellenistic Judaism." In *Civilizations of the Ancient Near East*, edited by Jack M. Sasson, 43–54. New York: Scribner.

Glassner, Jean-Jacques. 1995. "The Use of Knowledge in Ancient Mesopotamia." In *Civilizations of the Ancient Near East*, edited by Jack M. Sasson, 1815–23. New York: Scribner.

Gottwald, Norman. 1979a. "Sociological Method in the Study of Ancient Israel." In *Encounter with the Text: Form and History in the Hebrew Bible*, edited by M. J. Buss, 69–81. Missoula, MT: Scholars Press.

———. 1979b. *The Tribes of Yahweh: A Sociology of the Religion of Liberated Israel, 1250–1050 B.C.E.* Maryknoll, NY: Orbis.

Grabbe, Lester L. 2000. "Writing Israel's History at the End of the Twentieth Century." In *Congress Volume: Oslo 1998*, edited by André Lemaire and Magne Saebø, 203–18. Vetus Testamentum Supplement 80. Leiden: Brill.

———. 2003. "Introduction." In *"Like a Bird in a Cage": The Invasion of Sennacherib in 701 BCE*, edited by Lester L. Grabbe, 2–43. Journal for the Study of the Old Testament Supplement 363. New York: Sheffield Academic Press.

Graham, Brian. 2000. "The Past in Place: Historical Geographies of Identity." In *Modern Historical Geographies*, edited by Brian Graham and Catherine Nash, 70–99. London: Longman.

Graham, J. N. 1984. "'Vinedressers and Plowmen': 2 Kings 25:12 and Jeremiah 52:16." *Biblical Archaeologist* 47:55–58.

Grayson, Albert Kirk. 2004–5. "Shalmaneser III and the Levantine States: The 'Damascus Coalition.'" *Journal of Hebrew Scriptures* 5 (online at http://www.arts.ualberta.ca/JHS/Articles/article_34.htm).

Gunn, David M. 1999. "Narrative Criticism." In *To Each Its Own Meaning*, edited by Steven L. McKenzie and Stephen R. Haynes, 171–95. Louisville: Westminster/John Knox.

———. 2000. "Entertainment, Ideology, and the Reception of 'History': 'David's Jerusalem' as a Question of Space." In *"A Wise and Discerning Mind": Essays in Honor of Burke O. Long*, edited by Saul M. Olyan and Robert C. Culley, 153–61. Brown Judaic Studies 325. Providence, RI: Brown Judaic Studies.

Halligan, John M. 2002. "'Where Angels Fear to Tread . . .': An Account of the Development of the Social-Scientific Approach to the Study of the Ancient World." In *"Imagining" Biblical Worlds: Studies in Spatial, Social, and Historical Constructs in Honor of James W. Flanagan*, edited by David M. Gunn and Paula M. McNutt, 202–18. Journal for the Study of the Old Testament Supplement 359. New York: Sheffield Academic Press.

Hallo, William W., and K. Lawson Younger Jr., eds. 1997–2002. *The Context of Scripture*. 3 vols. Leiden: Brill.

Halpern, Baruch. 1988. *The First Historians: The Hebrew Bible and History*. San Francisco: Harper & Row.

———. 1999. "Erasing History: The Minimalist Assault on Ancient Israel." In *Israel's Past in Present Research*, edited by V. Phillips Long, 415–26. Winona Lake, IN: Eisenbrauns.

———. 2000. "The Gate of Megiddo and the Debate on the 10th Century." In *Congress Volume: Oslo 1998*, edited by André Lemaire and Magne Saebø, 79–121. Vetus Testamentum Supplement 80. Leiden: Brill.

Handy, Lowell K., ed. 2001. *The Age of Solomon: Scholarship at the Turn of the Millennium*. Leiden: Brill.

Hardin, J. W. 2004. "Understanding Domestic Space: An Example from Iron Age Tel Halif." *Near Eastern Archaeology* 67:71–83.

Harris, Marvin. 1979. *Cultural Materialism: The Struggle for a Science of Culture*. New York: Random.

Hedrick, Charles W., Jr. 2006. *Ancient History: Monuments and Documents*. Oxford: Blackwell.

Henige, David. 2005. "In Good Company: Problematic Sources and Biblical Historicity." *Journal for the Study of the Old Testament* 30:29–47.

Herion, Gary. 1986. "The Impact of Modern and Social Science Assumptions on the Reconstruction of Israelite History." *Journal for the Study of the Old Testament* 34:3–33.

Hoglund, K. G. 1997. "The Chronicler as Historian: A Comparativist Perspective." In *The Chronicler as Historian*, edited by M. Patrick Graham et al., 19–29. Journal for the Study of the Old Testament Supplement 238. Sheffield: Sheffield Academic Press.

Hopkins, David. 1985. *The Highlands of Canaan*. Sheffield: Almond.

———. 1987. "Life on the Land: The Subsistence Struggles of Early Israel." *Biblical Archaeologist* 50:178–91.

House, Paul R. 1992. "The Rise and Current Status of Literary Criticism of the Old Testament." In *Beyond Form Criticism: Essays in Old Testament Literary Criticism*, edited by Paul R. House, 3–22. Winona Lake, IN: Eisenbrauns.

Jackson, Kent P. 1989. "The Language of the Mesha Inscription." In *Studies in the Mesha Inscription and Moab*, edited by J. Andrew Dearman, 96–130. Atlanta: Scholars Press.

Jacoby, Ruth. 1991. "The Representations and Identification of Cities on Assyrian Reliefs." *Israel Exploration Journal* 41:112–31.

James, Simon. 1997. "Drawing Inferences: Visual Reconstructions in Theory and Practice." In *The Cultural Life of Images: Visual Representation in Archaeology*, edited by Brian L. Molyneaux, 22–48. London: Routledge.

James, T. G. H. 1984. *Pharaoh's People: Scenes from Life in Imperial Egypt*. Chicago: University of Chicago Press.

Japhet, Sara. 1993. *I and II Chronicles*. Old Testament Library. Louisville: Westminster/John Knox.

Jobling, David. 1995. "Structuralist Criticism: The Text's World of Meaning." In *Judges and Method*, edited by G. Yee, 91–118. Minneapolis: Fortress.

Jonker, Louis. 2000. "The Influence of Social Transformation on the Interpretation of the Bible: A Methodological Reflection." *Scriptura* 72:1–14.

Kallai, Zecharia. 1986. *Historical Geography of the Bible*. Jerusalem: Magnes.

Killebrew, Ann E. 2003. "Between Heaven and Earth: Educational Perspectives on the Archaeology and Material Culture of the Bible." In *Between Text and Artifact: Integrating Archaeology in Biblical Studies Teaching*, edited by Milton C. Moreland, 11–30. Atlanta: Society of Biblical Literature.

King, Philip J., and Lawrence G. Stager. 2002. *Life in Biblical Israel*. Louisville: Westminster/John Knox.

Kitchen, Kenneth A. 2004. *The Bible in Its World: The Bible and Archaeology Today*. London: Wipf & Stock.

Knight, Douglas, ed. 2004. *Methods of Biblical Interpretation*. Nashville: Abingdon.

Knoppers, Gary N. 1990. "Rehoboam in Chronicles: Villain or Victim?" *Journal of Biblical Literature* 109:423–40.

Koops, Robert. 1993. "Where Are We, Anyway? Space and Time Problems in 1 Samuel." *Bible Translator* 44:430–36.

Kuan, Jeffrey K. 1993. "Was Omri a Phoenician?" In *History and Interpretation: Essays in Honour of John H. Hayes*, edited by M. Patrick Graham et al., 231–44. Journal for the Study of the Old Testament Supplement 173. Sheffield: Sheffield Academic Press.

Laato, Antti. 2005. "Making History for Israel—Foundation, Blocking, and Policy." *Svensk exegetisk årsbok* 70:145–76.

Larsen, Mogens Trolle. 1995. "The 'Babel/Bible' Controversy and Its Aftermath." In *Civilizations of the Ancient Near East*, edited by Jack M. Sasson, 95–106. New York: Scribner.

Lemche, Niels P. 1988. *Ancient Israel: A New History of Israelite Society*. Sheffield: JSOT Press.

———. 1991. *The Canaanites and Their Land: The Tradition of the Canaanites*. Journal for the Study of the Old Testament Supplement 110. Sheffield: Sheffield Academic Press.

———. 1998. *The Israelites in History and Tradition*. Louisville: Westminster John Knox.

———. 2001. "Did Moses Speak Attic?" In *The Old Testament: A Hellenistic Book?*, edited by Niels Peter Lemche, 287–318. Sheffield: Sheffield Academic Press.

———. 2003. "On the Problem of Reconstructing Pre-Hellenistic Israelite (Palestinian) History." In *"Like a Bird in a Cage": The Invasion of Sennacherib in 701 BCE*, edited by Lester L. Grabbe, 150–67. Journal for the Study of the Old Testament Supplement 363. New York: Sheffield Academic Press.

Lenski, Gerhard, Patrick Nolan, and Jean Lenski. 1995. *Human Societies: An Introduction to Macrosociology*. 7th ed. New York: McGraw Hill.

Levin, Christoph. 1995. "Amos und Jerobeam I." *Vetus Testamentum* 45:307–17.

Lincoln, Bruce. 1994. *Authority: Construction and Corrosion*. Chicago: University of Chicago Press.

Linder, Elisha. 1992. "Excavating an Ancient Merchantman." *Biblical Archaeology Review* 18.6:24–35.

Linville, James R. 2000. "What Does 'It' Mean? Interpretation at the Point of No Return in Amos 1–2." *Biblical Interpretation* 8:400–424.

Long, V. Philips. 2002. "How Reliable Are Biblical Reports? Repeating Lester Grabbe's Comparative Experiment." *Vetus Testamentum* 52:367–84.

Luckenbill, D. D. 1968. *Ancient Records of Assyria and Babylonia*, vol. 2. Reprinted New York: Greenwood (orig. 1927).

Malina, Bruce J. 1982. "The Social Sciences and Biblical Interpretation." *Interpretation* 37:229–42.

Matthews, Victor H. 1986. "The Wells of Gerar." *Biblical Archaeologist* 49:118–26.

———. 1987. "Entrance Ways and Threshing Floors: Legally Significant Sites in the Ancient Near East." *Fides et historia* 19:25–40.

———. 1994. "Female Voices: Upholding the Honor of the Household." *Biblical Theology Bulletin* 24:8–15.

———. 1998. "Honor and Shame in Gender-Related Legal Situations in the Hebrew Bible." In *Gender and Law in the Hebrew Bible and the Ancient Near East*, edited by Victor H. Matthews et al., 97–112. Journal for the Study of the Old Testament Supplement 262. Sheffield: Sheffield Academic Press.

———. 2002a. *A Brief History of Ancient Israel*. Louisville: Westminster/ John Knox.

———. 2002b. "Syria to the Early Second Millennium." In *Mesopotamia and the Bible: Comparative Explorations*, edited by Mark W. Chavalas and K. Lawson Younger Jr., 168–90. Journal for the Study of the Old Testament Supplement 341. London: Sheffield Academic Press.

———. 2003a. "Physical Space, Imagined Space, and 'Lived Space' in Ancient Israel." *Biblical Theology Bulletin* 33:12–20.

———. 2003b. "Marriage and Family in the Ancient Near East." In *Marriage and Family in the Biblical World*, edited by Ken M. Campbell, 1–32. Downers Grove, IL: InterVarsity.

———. 2004a. "David and the Ark." *Bible Today* 42:143–47.

———. 2004b. *Judges and Ruth*. Cambridge: Cambridge University Press.

———. 2005. *Old Testament Turning Points: The Narratives That Shaped a Nation*. Grand Rapids: Baker Academic.

Matthews, Victor H., and Don C. Benjamin. 1993. *The Social World of Ancient Israel, 1250–587 BCE*. Peabody, MA: Hendrickson.

———. 1997. "Amnon and Tamar: A Matter of Honor (2 Sam 13:1–38)." In *Interconnections: A Festschrift in Honor of Michael Astour*, edited by Gordon D. Young, Mark W. Chavalas, and Richard E. Averbeck, 345–72. Baltimore: CDL.

————. 2006. *Old Testament Parallels: Laws and Stories from the Ancient Near East*. 3rd ed. Mahwah, NJ: Paulist Press.

Matthews, Victor H., and James C. Moyer. 2005. *The Old Testament: Text and Context*. 2nd ed. Peabody, MA: Hendrickson.

May, John. 1985. *Oxford Bible Atlas*. New York: Oxford University Press.

Mayes, Andrew D. H. 1989. *Old Testament in Sociological Perspective*. London: Marshall Pickering.

Mazar, Amihai. 1992. *Archaeology of the Land of the Bible*. New York: Doubleday.

————, ed. 2001. *Studies in the Archaeology of the Iron Age in Israel and Jordan*. Sheffield: Sheffield Academic Press.

Mazar, Amihai, David Amit, and Zvi Ilan. 1984. "The 'Border Road' between Michmash and Jericho and the Excavations at Horvat Shilhah." *Eretz-Israel* 17:236–50 (Hebrew).

Mazar, Benjamin. 1989. "The House of Omri." *Eretz-Israel* 20:215–19 (Hebrew).

McCarter, P. Kyle, Jr. 1984. *II Samuel*. Anchor Bible 9. New York: Doubleday.

McCutcheon, Russell T. 1999. "Introduction." In *The Insider/Outsider Problem in the Study of Religion*, edited by Russell T. McCutcheon, 1–18. London: Cassell.

McKenzie, Steven L., and Stephen R. Haynes, eds. 1999. *To Each Its Own Meaning*. Louisville: Westminster/John Knox.

McNutt, Paula M. 1999. *Reconstructing the Society of Ancient Israel*. Louisville: Westminster/John Knox.

Melugin, Roy F. 2003. "Recent Form Criticism Revisited in an Age of Reader Response." In *Changing Face of Form Criticism for the Twenty-first Century*, edited by Marvin A. Sweeney and Ehud Ben Zvi, 46–64. Grand Rapids: Eerdmans.

Merling, David. 2004. "The Relationship between Archaeology and the Bible: Expectations and Reality." In *The Future of Biblical Archaeology: Reassessing Methodologies and Assumptions*, edited by James K. Hoffmeier and Alan R. Millard, 29–42. Grand Rapids: Eerdmans.

Meyers, Carol L. 1983. "Procreation, Production, and Protection: Male-Female Balance in Early Israel." *Journal for the American Academy of Religion* 51:569–93.

————. 1988. *Discovering Eve: Ancient Israelite Women in Context*. New York: Oxford University Press.

———. 1991. "Of Drums and Damsels: Women's Performance in Ancient Israel." *Biblical Archaeologist* 54:16–27.

Millard, Alan R. 1994. "Story, History, and Theology." In *Faith, Tradition, and History: Old Testament Historiography in Its Ancient Near Eastern Context*, edited by Alan R. Millard, James K. Hoffmeier, and David W. Baker, 37–64. Winona Lake, IN: Eisenbrauns.

———. 1997. "Observations from the Eponym Lists." In *Assyria 1995*, edited by Simo Parpola and Robert M. Whiting, 207–15. Helsinki: Neo-Assyrian Text Corpus Project.

Miller, J. Maxwell. 1989. "Moab and the Moabites." In *Studies in the Mesha Inscription and Moab*, edited by J. Andrew Dearman, 1–40. Atlanta: Scholars Press.

———, ed. 1991a. *Archaeological Survey of the Kerak Plateau*. Atlanta: Scholars Press.

———. 1991b. "Is It Possible to Write a History of Israel without Relying on the Hebrew Bible?" In *The Fabric of History: Text, Artifact, and Israel's Past*, edited by Diana Edelman, 93–102. Sheffield: JSOT Press.

———. 2004. "History or Legend? Digging into Israel's Origins." *Christian Century* 121.4 (February 24): 42–47.

Miller, J. Maxwell, and John H. Hayes. 2006. *A History of Ancient Israel and Judah*. 2nd ed. Louisville: Westminster/John Knox.

Morrison, Martha. 1983. "The Jacob and Laban Narrative in Light of Near Eastern Sources." *Biblical Archaeologist* 46:155–64.

Moser, Stephanie, and Sam Smiles. 2005. "Introduction: The Image in Question." In *Envisioning the Past: Archaeology and the Image*, edited by Sam Smiles and Stephanie Moser, 1–12. Oxford: Blackwell.

Na'aman, Nadav. 1997. "King Mesha and the Foundation of the Moabite Monarchy." *Israel Exploration Journal* 47:83–92.

———. 1998. "Jehu Son of Omri: Legitimizing a Loyal Vassal by His Lord." *Israel Exploration Journal* 48:236–38.

Nelson, Richard D. 2002. *Deuteronomy*. Old Testament Library. Louisville: Westminster/John Knox.

Newcomb, Robert M. 1969. "Twelve Working Approaches to Historical Geography." *Yearbook of the Association of Pacific Coast Geographers* 31:27–50.

Newsom, Carol. 2001. "Probing Scripture: The New Biblical Critics." *Christian Century* 118.1 (January 3–10): 21–28.

Noort, E. 1997. "The Traditions of Ebal and Gerizim: Theological Positions in the Book of Joshua." In *Deuteronomy and Deuteronomistic*

Literature, edited by M. Vervenne and J. Lust, 161–80. Leuven: Leuven University Press.

Oded, Bustenay. 1992. *War, Peace, and Empire: Justifications for War in Assyrian Royal Inscriptions*. Wiesbaden: Reichert.

Olyan, Saul M. 1996. "Honor, Shame, and Covenant Relations in Ancient Israel and Its Environment." *Journal of Biblical Literature* 115:201–18.

Patterson, H. J., Donald J. Wiseman, and John J. Bimson. 1994. *New Bible Atlas*. Downers Grove, IL: InterVarsity.

Penchansky, David. 1992. "Up for Grabs: A Tentative Proposal for Doing Ideological Criticism." *Semeia* 59:35–41.

Pfeiffer, Charles F., E. Leslie Carlson, and Martin H. Scharlemann. 2003. *Baker's Bible Atlas*. Grand Rapids: Baker Academic.

Pike, Kenneth L. 1967. *Language in Relation to a Unified Theory of the Structure of Human Behavior*. 2nd ed. The Hague: Mouton.

Polzin, Robert. 1988. "On Taking Renewal Seriously: 1 Sam 11:1–15." In *Ascribe to the Lord: Biblical and Other Essays in Memory of Peter C. Craigie*, edited by Lyle Eslinger and Glen Taylor, 493–507. Journal for the Study of the Old Testament Supplement 67. Sheffield: JSOT Press.

Powell, J. M. 2000. "Historical Geographies of the Environment." In *Modern Historical Geographies*, edited by Brian Graham and Catherine Nash, 169–92. London: Longman.

Pritchard, James, ed. 1969. *Ancient Near Eastern Texts Relating to the Old Testament*. 3rd ed. Princeton: Princeton University Press.

———. 1997. *HarperCollins Concise Atlas of the Bible*. San Francisco: Harper-Collins.

Provan, Iain W., V. Philips Long, and Tremper Longman III. 2003. *A Biblical History of Israel*. Louisville: Westminster/John Knox.

Radcliffe-Brown, A. R. 1952. *Structure and Function in Primitive Society*. New York: Free Press.

Rainey, Anson F., and R. Steven Notley. 2006. *The Sacred Bridge: Carta's Atlas of the Biblical World*. Jerusalem: Carta.

Rasmussen, Carl G. 1989. *Zondervan NIV Atlas of the Bible*. Grand Rapids: Zondervan.

Redford, Donald B. 1992. *Egypt, Canaan, and Israel in Ancient Times*. Princeton: Princeton University Press.

Reid, Garnett H. 1998. "Minimalism and Biblical History." *Bibliotheca sacra* 155:394–410.

Ricoeur, Paul. 1995. *Figuring the Sacred: Religion, Narrative, and the Imagi-nation*. Translated by David Pellauer. Edited by Mark I. Wallace. Minneapolis: Fortress.

Rogerson, John. 1985. *Atlas of the Bible*. New York: Facts on File.

Rubin, Rehav. 1990. "Historical Geography of Eretz-Israel: Survey of the Ancient Period." In *The Land That Became Israel: Studies in Historical Geography*, edited by Ruth Kark, 23–36. New Haven: Yale University Press.

Sahlins, Marshall. 1972. *Stone Age Economics*. Chicago: Aldine-Atherton.

Sasson, Jack M. 1981. "On Choosing Models for Recreating Israelite Pre-Monarchic History." *Journal for the Study of the Old Testament* 21:3–24.

———. 1982. "Accounting Discrepancies in the Mari NI.GUB [NÍG.DU] Texts." In *Zikir Šumim: Assyriological Studies Presented to F. R. Kraus*, edited by G. van Driel et al., 326–41. Leiden: Brill.

Schottroff, Luise, et al., eds. 1998. *Feminist Interpretation: The Bible in Women's Perspective*. Minneapolis: Fortress.

Seymour, Susanne. 2000. "Historical Geographies of Landscape." In *Modern Historical Geographies*, edited by Brian Graham and Catherine Nash, 193–217. London: Longman.

Smelik, Klaas A. D. 1990. "The Literary Structure of King Mesha's Inscription." *Journal for the Study of the Old Testament* 46:21–30.

Soggin, J. Alberto. 1984. *A History of Ancient Israel*. Translated by John Bowden. Philadelphia: Westminster.

Sommer, B. D. 2006. "The Source Critic and the Religious Interpreter." *Interpretation* 60:9–21.

Stager, Lawrence E. 1985. "The Archaeology of the Family." *Bulletin of the American Schools of Oriental Research* 260:1–35.

———. 1990. "Shemer's Estate." *Bulletin of the American Schools of Oriental Research* 277–278:93–107.

Stansell, Gary. 1999. "The Gift in Ancient Israel." *Semeia* 87:65–90.

Steinberg, Naomi. 1993. *Kinship and Marriage in Genesis: A Household Economics Perspective*. Minneapolis: Fortress.

Stieglitz, Robert R. 1984. "Long-Distance Seafaring in the Ancient Near East." *Biblical Archaeologist* 47:134–42.

Stone, L. G. 1979. "The Revival of Narrative: Reflections on a New Old History." *Past and Present* 85:3–24.

———. 1997. "Redaction Criticism: Whence, Whither, and Why? or, Going beyond Source and Form Criticism without Leaving Them Behind."

In *A Biblical Itinerary*, edited by Eugene E. Carpenter, 77–90. Journal for the Study of the Old Testament Supplement 240. Sheffield: Sheffield Academic Press.

Stuart, Douglas. 1987. *Hosea–Jonah*. Word Biblical Commentary 31. Waco: Word.

Svensson, Jan. 1994. *Towns and Toponyms in the Old Testament with Special Emphasis on Joshua 14–21*. Coniectanea biblica: Old Testament Series 38. Stockholm: Almqvist & Wiksell.

Sweeney, Marvin A., and Ehud Ben Zvi, eds. 2003. *The Changing Face of Form Criticism for the Twenty-First Century*. Grand Rapids: Eerdmans.

Tadmor, Hayim. 1975. "Assyria and the West: The Ninth Century and Its Aftermath." In *Unity and Diversity*, edited by Hans Goedicke and J. J. M. Roberts, 36–48. Baltimore: Johns Hopkins University Press.

Talmon, Shemaryahu. 1978. "The Comparative Method in Biblical Interpretation: Principles and Problems." In *Congress Volume: Göttingen 1977*, 320–56. Vetus Testamentum Supplement 29. Leiden: Brill.

Tate, W. Randolph. 2006. *Interpreting the Bible: A Handbook of Terms and Methods*. Peabody, MA: Hendrickson.

Thompson, Thomas L. 1992. *Early History of the Israelite People: From Written and Archaeological Sources*. Leiden: Brill.

———. 2005. "The Role of Faith in Historical Research." *Scandinavian Journal of the Old Testament* 19:111–34.

Throntveit, Mark A. 1997. "The Chronicler's Speeches and Historical Reconstruction." In *The Chronicler as Historian*, edited by M. Patrick Graham et al., 225–45. Journal for the Study of the Old Testament Supplement 238. Sheffield: Sheffield Academic Press.

Tov, Emanuel. 2001. *Text Criticism of the Hebrew Bible*. 2nd ed. Minneapolis: Fortress.

Ussishkin, David. 1977. "The Destruction of Lachish by Sennacherib and the Dating of the Royal Judean Storage Jars." *Tel Aviv* 4:28–60.

———. 1979. "The 'Lachish Reliefs' and the City of Lachish." *Israel Exploration Journal* 29:174–95.

———. 1997a. "Lachish." In *The Oxford Encyclopedia of Archaeology in the Near East*, edited by Eric M. Meyers, 3.317–23. New York: Oxford University Press.

———. 1997b. "Jezreel, Samaria, and Megiddo: Royal Centres of Omri and Ahab." In *Congress Volume: Cambridge 1995*, edited by J. A. Emerton, 351–64. Leiden: Brill.

Van Seters, John. 1983. *In Search of History: Historiography and the Origins of Biblical History*. New Haven: Yale University Press.

Vaughn, Andrew G. 1999. *Theology, History, and Archaeology in the Chronicler's Account of Hezekiah*. Atlanta: Scholars Press.

Vaughn, Andrew G., and Christopher A. Rollston. 2005. "The Antiquities Market, Sensationalized Textual Data, and Modern Forgeries." *Near Eastern Archaeology* 68:61–68.

Wallace, Howard N. 1986. "The Oracles against the Israelite Dynasties in 1 and 2 Kings." *Biblica* 67:21–40.

Weinstock, Leo I. 1983. "Sound and Meaning in Biblical Hebrew." *Journal of Semitic Studies* 28:49–62.

Whitelam, Keith W. 1996. *The Invention of Ancient Israel: The Silencing of Palestinian History*. New York: Routledge.

Williamson, H. G. M. 1995. "Sound, Sense, and Language in Isaiah 24–27." *Journal of Jewish Studies* 46:1–9.

Willis, John T. 1985. "Dialogue between Prophet and Audience as a Rhetorical Device in the Book of Jeremiah." *Journal for the Study of the Old Testament* 33:63–82.

Willis, Timothy M. 2001. *The Elders of the City: A Study of the Elders-Laws in Deuteronomy*. Atlanta: Society of Biblical Literature.

Winter, Irene J. 1981. "Royal Rhetoric and Development of Historical Narrative in Neo-Assyrian Reliefs." *Studies in Visual Communication* 7.2:2–38.

Wolff, Hans W. 1974. *Hosea*. Translated by Gary Stansell. Edited by Paul D. Hanson. Hermeneia. Philadelphia: Fortress.

Yarchin, William. 2004. *History of Biblical Interpretation: A Reader*. Peabody, MA: Hendrickson.

Yasur-Landau, Assaf. 2005. "Old Wine in New Vessels: Intercultural Contact, Innovation, and Aegean, Canaanite, and Philistine Foodways." *Tel Aviv* 32:168–91.

Yee, Gale A. 2003. *Poor Banished Children of Eve: Woman as Evil in the Hebrew Bible*. Minneapolis: Fortress.

Younger, K. Lawson, Jr. 1990. *Ancient Conquest Accounts: A Study in Ancient Near Eastern and Biblical History Writing*. Journal for the Study of the Old Testament Supplement 98. Sheffield: JSOT Press.

Zevit, Ziony. 2002. "Three Debates about Bible and Archaeology." *Biblica* 83:1–27.

Subject Index

Ancient Writings Index

225